TIME MANAGEMENT

Advance Praise for *Time Management*

'This book recommends techniques devised and utilized by highly successful and effective people, and helps readers learn to prioritize internal fulfillment to obtain internal satisfaction. Through the use of yoga wisdom, intriguing stories and daily examples, readers will learn to successfully balance time spent on one's work with interpersonal growth and spiritual fulfillment. The book identifies the most common obstacles encountered in fulfilling responsibilities and how to successfully overcome them through determination, preparation and patience. By reading about failures of successful inventors, the reader will also learn to view failure as a necessary step towards success. And by utilizing the effective time management strategies recommended, readers will have the tools necessary to master the art of time management.'

—Adria C. Savino, MD, addiction psychiatrist

'The author discusses time management and goal setting through the Eisenhower Decision Matrix and the twenty-first century three-dimensional matrix, and emphasizes aligning goals with our values and balancing different aspects of life. The book also explores the idea of true happiness through controlling the mind and aligning goals with ultimate happiness, citing ancient texts that equate our mind and senses with wild horses. The author discusses the importance of being mindful of resource needs for sustained growth and the need for suitable systems to address disorganization. He also emphasizes the need to develop internally to achieve goals, including replacing negative self-talk with practical thinking, combined with hard work and perseverance. Additionally, it highlights the importance of both internal and external adjustments to improve time management and the significance of identifying the most important task (MIT) to achieve top-priority goals. Personally, I learned that time management is not simply the management of time, but the management of what we choose to do with our precious time. As someone who tends to multitask occasionally, I found some of the skills mentioned in the book to be useful. This past week, for example, I stopped multitasking and found myself able to focus better on several tasks that I had to do.'

—Padmaja Puppala, MD, addiction psychiatrist

'I really liked the Pomodoro principle and customization of it to suit one's personal needs, monk's lotus leaf technique, the 80–20 principles and the principles of communication in our daily lives. This has shed light on common time-wasting actions, and I have decided to consciously avoid them. PASTA logic and various keys to fine-tune and improve one's efficiency and will benefit every reader. I am confident this book will benefit not only professionals and youths but all sections of society. I strongly recommend this book to everyone for their self-mastery.'

—Dan Fink , MD, occupational and environmental medicine physician

TIME MANAGEMENT

A MONK'S WISDOM FOR PERSONAL FULFILLMENT AND PROFESSIONAL ACHIEVEMENT

Yugal Kishore Das

HARPER VANTAGE

HarperCollins *Publishers* India

First published in India in 2023 by Harper Vantage
An imprint of HarperCollins *Publishers*
4th Floor, Tower A, Building No. 10, DLF Cyber City,
DLF Phase II, Gurugram, Haryana – 122002
www.harpercollins.co.in

2 4 6 8 10 9 7 5 3 1

P-ISBN: 978-93-5699-938-1
E-ISBN: 978-93-5699-387-7

Typeset in 12/15.7 Palatino Linotype at
Manipal Technologies Limited, Manipal

Printed and bound at
Thomson Press (India) Ltd

MIX
Paper from responsible sources
FSC® C010615

This book is produced from independently certified FSC® paper to ensure responsible forest management.

To my dear spiritual master,
H.H. Radhanath Swami

Contents

Foreword

The Art and Science of Self-Mastery by my dear friend, Yugal Kishore Das, presents practical insights into stress, anger and time management. By combining powerful stories with life lessons, illustrations to reflect and remember, and questions at the end of each chapter to help you on a sincere journey towards self-mastery, Das offers a pragmatic guide to enhance your professional and personal lives. Grounded in the foundations of Vedic wisdom, Das comes up with a handy manual that allows us to look into our inner mirror. Covered by the dust of our imperfections—anger, greed, envy and pride—we are unable to see our reflections clearly in that mirror. Das offers valuable tools to clean this mirror so we can see ourselves clearly.

In the summer of 2022, I was approached by Dr Ramana Vinjamuri, our common friend and well-wisher, to write the foreword for this important contribution. Vinjamuri described the significance and the practical wisdom offered in these books for each and everyone of us. Inspired by our conversation, I quickly took to reading the manuscripts and could not put them down. Having been thus exhilarated, I found immense pleasure in writing this foreword.

I have known Yugal Kishore Das for more than twenty years. When I first met him, he was working as a software consultant with MetLife insurance company in Albany, New York. He would help arrange programmes for me in Albany. I would stay at his house during weekends. This programme eventually shaped into a university programme where we were preaching to the students at State University of New York, Albany. Many students were benefitted from this programme. This engagement made us good friends. He eventually received initiation from my spiritual master and became my spiritual brother and this brought us closer. He would regularly come to our monastery in Manhattan to understand the life of a monk. In that association, he felt that human life is meant for self-realization and this can be attained by selflessly serving humanity. This eventually led him to give up his job and join a monastery in West Virginia. I really appreciated his courage and sacrifice. He sacrificed his job and life for the benefit of others. Time and distance have not proved to be obstacles in our brotherhood. We regularly preached together on several occasions. He started extensively travelling and preaching the message all over America. It is for the benefit of the people that he writes these books.

There was once a retreat in Palace of Gold in West Virginia which I attended with other monks in our monastery. There was a discussion on the causes of various problems of the world. I remember Yugal Kishore Das saying that envy, anger and greed are the problems of mankind and by practising spirituality sincerely, one can eventually become free from these unwanted impurities of the heart. External problems are the outcome of internal problems. It was a lively discussion and other monks also shared their perspectives on the problems of the world. Why are oceans and rivers polluted? It is because every heart is polluted. Since the population is very large, this inner pollution would naturally reflect in rivers and oceans in a big way. So, ecological problems have a connection with the lack of spirituality in society and real spirituality must focus on cleansing the heart with an aim to leading a pure life. That way the world will become a better place to live in for everyone.

We met many times in this way and shared and expressed our opinions. Whenever we met, we would sit together and meditate for hours in the mornings. This has helped develop a camaraderie between us. I strongly feel this book will be beneficial to many as he has shared his valuable realizations and experiences.

There are three books in this series: *Stress Management, Anger Management* and *Time Management*. Each of these books is self-contained and written in an easy-to-understand manner with practical and eye-opening lessons embedded in each chapter. Each chapter ends with few questions that make you think and explore your inner self. The author has penned these parts and chapters in such a way that the reader can turn to any page and find something meaningful and pragmatic. By encouraging you to remember and recollect what you have read in the text, the illustrations help guide you further.

In *Time Management,* Yugal Kishore Das, emphasizing the importance of how time is precious, shares key principles of time management and why we need to manage our time, as well as the kind of obstacles that hinder us when we put these principles to practice. This is where we realize why we are unable to implement these familiar yet fruitful practices into our routines. The simplicity and clarity with which these tips are described will encourage each one of us to implement them in our daily lives and benefit from the author's wisdom.

In *Anger Management*, the author starts by describing the nuts and bolts of anger. The readers will be pleasantly surprised with insightful lessons where the author reveals how our anger shuts off our intelligence and acts against us. When we reach the peak of heightened anger in the spur of a moment, what we never think of are the consequences of our actions taken during those weak moments. If we are aware of these consequences, we would at least think before taking any action. The author takes a holistic approach on how we can prevent anger by understanding our inner self, our lifestyle and our thought process. Das closes this part with some sensible techniques on anger management. By presenting simple formulas and equations, he reveals our inner psyche. For example, the author talks about 7–38–55 rule in effective communication where it is not simply about our words. Only 7 per cent is the choice of words, 38 per cent is tone of voice and a majority, 55 per cent is our body language. Our body language and tone depend on our mood and mentality. The author guides us on nourishing and nurturing our inner self to groom our mood and mentality.

In *Stress Management,* Das begins with a touching story of his interaction with a student. Just with this one incident, I am confident that the readers can relate to and understand that stress is part of everyone's dictionary. He explains the fundamentals of stress and different stressors—knowledge derived from Vedic wisdom. He further talks about the lifecycle of stress. Awareness about these topics somehow brings a sense of calmness within us. Perhaps because we are able to understand that we are not the only ones stressed out and it gives out the hope that even if we are in the dark now, there will be light sooner than later. In the next chapters, Das gets into the details of the internal and external factors of stress and how these affect our body and mind. At this point, instead of stressing on stress, he takes us on an uplifting and optimistic journey on how we can avoid stress, and suggests some preventive measures using the principles of effective communication and anxiety management. Finally, he closes by presenting a practical skill set on how to manage stress. These are some of my favourite parts of the book as they present methods on how to practise forgiveness, gratitude and service. The readers are left at this point with key practices on relaxation, meditation and prayer.

In summary, I am confident that you will learn meaningful lessons in every page of this book just as I did. I encourage you to use these lessons, respond to the questions he poses at the end of each chapter, remember the tips and reflect on them, and, finally, adapt and apply them in your personal and professional lives.

As a techie, as a software engineer working for multinational companies, as a counsellor, as a life coach and as a monk in the West, Yugal Kishore Das had trekked a unique journey. From this unique journey comes his unique insights into the inner engineering that enables each one of us to turn our weaknesses such as anger, stress, sense of inferiority and procrastination into our strengths such as inner peace, composure, determination and confidence.

Pandit Dasa
mindful leadership expert and
motivational speaker,
USA Today's 'Top 8 Influential Speakers to
Follow' in 2002,
author of bestsellers *Urban Monk* and
Closing the Apps
For more information, please
visit: www.panditdasa.com

Preface

Usually, it is medical doctors and research scientists who write books on such topics. So, what made me (a monk) write these books?

As technology started developing with a singular motive to make our lives better, paradoxically and interestingly, our lives started becoming more and more mechanical. Despite technology being at its peak today, we all have become very disoriented in our lives. In the US alone, an astounding number of people have mental health problems. We live in times of a lot of social unrest.

Why is there so much social unrest globally? It is because everyone is experiencing a lot of internal unrest, one within themselves. Why is there this unrest at an individual and internal level? When we face disturbance on a physical, mental or emotional level, it disturbs or inner peace. Apart from this, nature too offers us challenges in the form of extreme weather, cyclones, floods, earthquakes and tsunamis, etc. In this world where everyone is quarrelling with each other, there is always somebody or something that seems to disturb our peace. Mental and physical ailments also cause us a lot of stress. Apart from this, the world of today is becoming increasingly global. Hence, a slight disturbance caused in one part of the world spirals out to affect people in the other part of the world, making them frustrated and depressed. Stress, anxiety, frustration and depression have become the buzz words in this busy world.

Managing our stress, anger and time on a daily basis has become especially difficult. Everyone seems to be extremely busy. But by the end of the hectic day, they realize that they have truly accomplished only a little. This makes them unhappy.

Stress is a common problem in society. We all have a list of things to address. Some demand our immediate attention. But we may not have enough resources to manage these tasks or to deal with the resultant stress.

When we are busy addressing and sorting out everyday problems all the time, our body finds itself constantly in the fight-and-flight mode, with very little rest. In such a state, things are bound to go wrong, and, as a result, we also become angry.

How do we make ourselves immune to all these problems? That is the subject matter of these books. For example, we must understand that we have no control over tomorrow's weather or how our boss is going to act with us, but we have control over how *we* react. By developing the right mindset and/or by taking precautionary measures, we can either minimize the problem or totally avoid the problem. For example, if the tree is healthy and strong and firmly rooted deep within the soil, it can weather any type of storms or overcome threats posed by any type of pests. In the same way, if we can become strong and firm, we can face the storms of life. What are the tools we need to make us firmly rooted within ourselves to face any type of disturbance or adversity in our lives?

I write these books to equip people with the necessary tools needed to deal with the common problems of life that we all face on a day-to-day basis. First step in that direction is awareness and acceptance of the problems, and recognizing the need to address them. Of course, for that to happen, we need to have a very good understanding of our mind and sense organs, and their collective functioning in both relaxed as well as problematic environments.

Since the mind, as opposed to the brain, is not a physical organ but a very intangible one, its behaviour is unpredictable and differs from individual to individual. Once, I was conducting a seminar in a college on the positive attitude of the mind. After the seminar, a student came to me and said, 'If only you had come two weeks ago and conducted this seminar, my friend would not have committed suicide.' Moved, I asked him why he felt like that. He said, the presentation was mentally very uplifting and gave so much hope and strength to deal with the problems of life.

During my research, I was fascinated to find how our mind operates differently at different times and different environments. It is very interesting to note that our mind picks up all of the information that we gullibly and inadvertently collect through our various experiences. But when we want to erase it from our mind, it is not easy to erase them. These thoughts circulate in our minds for a very long time. I tried to find the relation between the nature around us, our impulsive thoughts and the reactions of the body to them. The reality is our senses constantly demand enjoyment. But our mind being connected to our senses has the ability control them. However, the mind is fickle and gets distracted easily, without bothering about the consequences. This is a serious problem, and many people are not aware of this problem. Intelligence is superior to the mind and hence can control the senses. If we can sharpen our intelligence and control the mind, our life becomes much better. In fact, learning this truth led me to take up the meditation process more seriously, whereby I tried to restrain the demands of the mind and the senses with a sharpened intelligence.

I have been meditating for more than twenty-five years on a daily basis. I am myself fascinated with the results. I was part of Henry Ford Hospital research team which conducted research on the efficacy of mantra meditation (where you meditate by chanting on a mantra) and its effect on the brain. Based on my experience in dealing with the mind, I have developed a few tools and a lifestyle whereby one can handle anxiety and stress. With these tools, I have been counselling hundreds of professionals from the corporate world, as well as many families and students for more than twenty-one years in the US and other countries, and have helped them cope with stress, anxiety, anger and depression.

My training is based on imparting knowledge on the internal aspects of our physical bodies—their functioning and their inter-relationships.

I provide separate tools to handle the physical body, the internal space of the mind and the deeper intellect. When we realize that we, as consciousness, are different from our physical organs and that it is our thoughts that lead us to action, we become careful with our thought process. This is where we need help and training. With proper guidance and practice, we can alter various negative patterns of our mind to positive patterns, and bring a revolutionary change in our actions and in our lives.

I have mentioned many examples and case studies in these books for the benefit of the reader. If you are able to get some benefit out of them, I will be most happy as a monk and consider this little endeavour fruitful.

Your humble servant,
Yugal Kishore Das
Michigan (USA), 17 July 2023

Introduction

Time is precious. As Geoffrey Chaucer put it, 'Time and tide wait for no man.' Without our knowledge, time is continuously slipping from our hands. But despite its transience, time is a powerful force. If we don't learn how to use it to our advantage, it can destroy us. After all, our time in this world is temporary. If we do not properly manage the time allotted to us, all our efforts to effect change in our lives and the lives of others will prove fruitless. We always see people running around trying to get things done, but at the end of the day we often hear them say that they have accomplished very little. 'There simply isn't enough time in the day,' they may claim. The fact is that time management is an art. By mastering it, one can sculpt a beautiful life for oneself and add a special vibrancy to the lives of others.

This book covers the following topics:

- What is time management?
- Why do we need time management?
- What obstacles get in the way of proper time management?
- What effective techniques enhance our time management?

CHAPTER 1

The Most Sought-after and Least-cherished Commodity

Time is not a renewable resource. No amount of wealth could ever give us the power to 'buy' back even a moment of time lost. Yesterday is gone, forever out of reach. Despite how obvious this fact may seem, we generally don't realize it until later in life. Without such foresight, we're prone to waste a vast amount of precious time on social media, gossip, fighting over trivial issues and so on. In this way, many people watch the years slip away, never realizing that their most precious resource is rapidly getting depleted.

This brings to mind an interesting phenomenon you may consider worthy of note. In our youth, we generally have both good health and lots of time, but no wealth. In adulthood, most of us accrue a comfortable amount of wealth and continue to enjoy decent health, but, given work and family obligations, we have no time. Finally, in old age, especially after retirement, we have time to enjoy the solid nest egg we've built up, but our health is now poor from years of hard work. Conflicted, we try to regain our health by spending huge sums of money on medical treatments. Our time and wealth are sapped in this cycle of ill health, treatment and recuperation, and we finally find that all three assets—health, wealth and time—have been depleted beyond recovery.

My monk friend Sutapa condensed this conundrum into the phrase 'hurry, worry, sorry'. In youth, hurry is the ringleader; we feel the need to go, go, go, to achieve lots of things and prove ourselves to the world. In adulthood, worry takes over; we may still desire to achieve a lot but, alas, half our life has already passed and time is running out! Finally, in old age, we feel regret over the things we failed to achieve and the mistakes we made in our endeavours to achieve them. By this point, it's too late to start anew; we can only lament our wayward attempts in the past. As a result, many pass through life not really *living* at all, only anxiously racing against the clock and ultimately losing in the end.

Anyone who makes their career the focal point of their life is often baffled upon retirement. They

generally end up passing their days in loneliness. With no career left to meditate upon, their anxiety shifts to their own body, which is now noticeably decaying as the days pass by. Such lamentation, however, would never befall them if they knew of the intrinsic treasure buried within their heart. Instead, they'd look at their final chapter as a golden opportunity to unearth the infinite wealth lying dormant within.

1.1. ALEXANDER'S FINAL DECLARATION

Regarding what should be our main focus and what should be secondary, we can take a cue from the last three dying wishes of the world's most renowned conqueror, Alexander the Great.[1]

1 Prakash Joshi Pax, 'Why Alexander the Great Made These 3 Strange Wishes in His Deathbed', Medium.com, 17 January 2021, https://medium.com/lessons-from-history/why-alexander-the-great-made-these-3-strange-wishes-in-his-deathbed-ed7712af985d

Upon returning from what would turn out to be his final battle, Alexander fell horribly ill. Despite the best medicine and treatment the world could offer, his health rapidly declined. Realizing that his death was imminent, the great king made his final requests known.

First, he desired that his coffin be carried by his doctors alone—no generals, no royalty, only his medical attendants. Second, he requested that all the silver and gold he had acquired in his wildly successful campaigns be strewn upon the dirt path leading to his tomb. Finally, he asked for his hands to be placed outside his coffin for all to see.

When one of his dear commanders tearfully asked him to explain his bizarre final wishes, he responded with a unique set of reasons. Having doctors carry his coffin would convey that, no matter how skilful they were or how many resources they may have had at their disposal, *no one* could stop death. Strewing silver and gold upon the path to his tomb was a way of posing a question: although he had amassed more wealth than anyone in history, '... if even my fortune cannot save me from death or extend my life by one breath, then what is wealth's *actual* value?' Finally, his exposed hands would signify to the world that, just as he had arrived in it empty-handed, he would now be forced to leave the world, *his* world, so to speak, with absolutely nothing.

In other words, no matter how much wealth we amass or how many resources are at our disposal, our presence in this world is temporary. We should always prioritize internal fulfillment instead of attempting to satisfy ourselves with things that will ultimately be ripped away from us regardless of how successfully we may have acquired them.

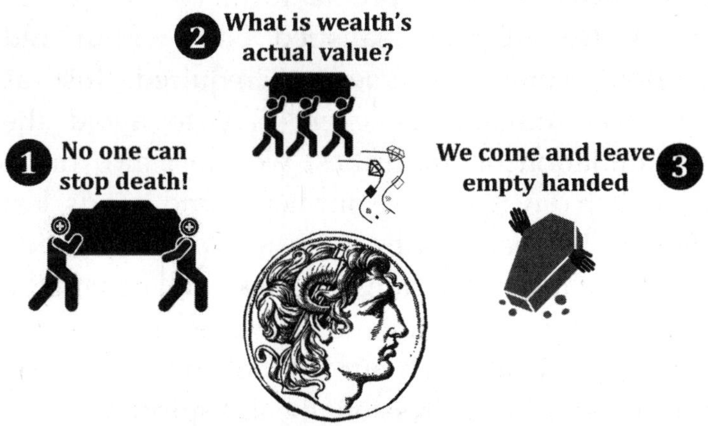

1.2. THE ULTIMATE SUCCESS

Time can only be a valuable asset if it provides us opportunities to achieve true fulfillment. Alexander informed us that material success is limited, as it is doomed to disintegrate before the onslaught of time. The solution is to mould life so as to achieve a state of inner satisfaction and bliss. These are assets we can carry with us throughout life, irrespective of what happens externally, and it is this internal fulfillment that we will take with us after death. This process of internal development entails cultivating a sharp and steady mind that can discern between those things that actually contribute to our ultimate success and those that are ultimately a waste of time.

To achieve the supreme form of success, in which we are fully satisfied both within and without, some refinement is required. Just as we clean our bodies every day to avoid the accumulation of impurities, we must also make time each day to cleanse our hearts and minds, lest they too be overcome by pollution. With a purified heart, whatever decisions we make will benefit the whole world. Let's take a look at a few systems that allow us to reach our full holistic potential—interpersonally, professionally and spiritually.

1.3. MAKE THE MOST OF YOUR TIME

In short, time management is not simply the management of time, but the management of what we choose to do with our precious time.

There is a seemingly infinite number of things we can choose to do with our time. Usually, we choose to do the things we feel are most urgent or those that we feel give us the greatest sense of satisfaction. Many consider the pursuit of money a reasonable way to spend most of their time; others prefer to enjoy sensual pleasures all day. Often, we find ourselves feeling that we've wasted our time doing something that initially seemed like a valuable pursuit but in the end turned out to be a sham. So how are we to make sure that we're spending our time properly?

1.4. BIG ROCKS FIRST

In some of our spiritual leadership schools, we ask the children to imagine a glass jar being filled to the top with big rocks, small pebbles, sand and water. We then ask them the order in which the different materials should be added to properly accommodate all of them.

After some deliberation, most kids answer correctly: big rocks first, then small pebbles, then the sand and finally the water—a perfect fit! The big rocks leave lots of crevices for the pebbles to fall into and the sand then finds its way into the even smaller crevices that remain. Water can find space amidst all the solids, and with that the project is complete. However, if even one element of the experiment is inserted in the wrong order, an overflow is inevitable. What this tells us is that prioritization is paramount. The first principle of time management can be derived from this experiment: *big rocks first*—the top of our to-do list should always be reserved for the most important tasks.

1.5. THE EISENHOWER DECISION MATRIX: TIME MANAGEMENT CODE

An easy way to ensure that the big rocks are always inserted first is to employ the Eisenhower decision matrix, a tool used by former U.S. President Dwight D. Eisenhower and popularized by Stephen Covey in his famous book *The Seven Habits of Highly Effective People*. This tool forces us to identify tasks and sort them according to their respective levels of importance and urgency.

Not every time-sensitive task is equally important, and not all important tasks need be done immediately. By classifying our to-do items according to their degrees of importance and

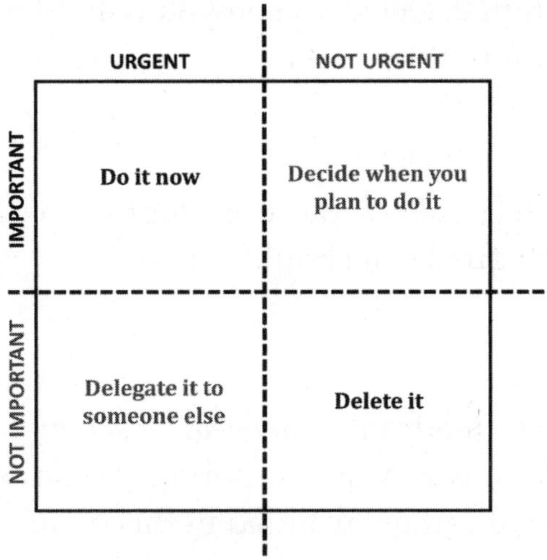

urgency, we can accurately assess which ones require our immediate attention (the big rocks) and which can (and should) wait. Try it out:

Draw a to-do list that has four quadrants, each large enough to write tasks in. Label them as follows:

Quadrant 1: Urgent & Important

Quadrant 2: Important & Not Urgent

Quadrant 3: Urgent & Not Important

Quadrant 4: Not Important & Not Urgent

Next, mark each quadrant using the 4D formula: Do, Decide, Delegate, Delete.

Quadrant 1: Do it now

Quadrant 2: Decide when you will do it

Quadrant 3: Delegate it to someone else if possible

Quadrant 4: Delete it

Now, let's take a more in-depth look at what tasks each quadrant should consist of.

Quadrant 1

This is the quadrant of *immediate action,* for tasks that are both urgent and important. Some examples of tasks that can be included in this quadrant are:

- Preparing for an exam or job interview that's taking place the following day
- Repairing a car part that could cause serious problems if driven without having been looked at
- Fixing your company's software program failure
- Tending to some kind of injury or health issue

What is common to all the above tasks is that not performing them will result in negative consequences.

It is very important, however, to be able to clearly discern what belongs in this immediate action quadrant and what does not. Those who view everything as an immediate action item inevitably burn out. These are the folks you see running around with a perpetual air of doom and gloom about them, always bogged down by stress and anxiety. Ironically, in their manic scrambling to get everything done, they often fail to accomplish important things due to a lack of time. Their output, though voluminous, is often of poor quality.

Don't be a firefighting manager. Be sensible in your assessment of what absolutely needs to get done now based on urgency and importance and delay or delegate the rest.

Quadrant 2

This is the quadrant of *grade,* for important activities that are not necessarily urgent. Some examples of tasks that can be included in it are:

- Planning for a business trip that is a month away
- Preparing for a job interview that is two weeks away
- Studying for an exam that is a month away

- Booking hotel rooms and travel arrangements for a family trip that is two months away

In other words, these tasks must be tended to soon but not necessarily today.

Despite the eminent importance of the first quadrant, the real key to successful time management is how one approaches quadrant 2. It is this quadrant in which one sets oneself up for long-term success. This is the space in which we work towards goals, invest in relationships, balance our work and leisure and plan for important events down the line. The most successful managers give special attention to this quadrant, aware that it is only a matter of time before the things listed in it become both important *and* urgent. By investing time and energy in this quadrant according to one's schedule, one ensures anxiety-free and abundant long-term returns.

Quadrant 3

This is the quadrant of *duplicity*, for urgent activities that aren't so important. These tasks are time-sensitive and demand immediate attention but aren't essential to one's long-term success. Some examples of tasks that can be included in it are:

- Trivial texts
- Social media interactions
- Flash sales
- Getting involved in an argument with co-workers

Our mind may claim otherwise, but such tasks are usually fruitless distractions. This quadrant is filled with to-do items related to our phone, which enter our consciousness by way of a notification that seems important but is actually of little consequence. Even important phone calls tend to drift into gossip and senseless talk after the initial points have been made. Deceptively, however, people often convince themselves that such activities are of the utmost importance. Being absorbed in non-essential activities, such people achieve very little. Being overly concerned with 'the talk of the town', they tend to become somewhat docile, moulding their lives to what they perceive will garner them the most admiration. In such a state, they become doormats to others, accepting whatever comes their way without actively pursuing their innermost dreams. Being overly concerned with their image, they fail to realize that they are painting a picture that they themselves do not like. Their hurrying around thus ultimately cedes ground to feelings of regret over time wasted catering to others' thoughts and desires instead of their own.

Quadrant 4

This is the quadrant of *waste,* for activities that are both unimportant and not urgent. These activities are a waste of time from beginning to end; they do not contribute to our overall progress in any tangible way. Endless scrolling, non-stop streaming, senseless internet browsing and the like are examples of activities that can be included in this quadrant. People who regularly become too absorbed in the activities of this quadrant are typically unreliable escapists. Overly laidback, such people just want to enjoy non-stop. They ignore the importance of sacrificing some immediate enjoyment for their own ultimate good. Being averse to hard work, they shudder at any form of responsibility. If they have dreams, those dreams remain dreams forever. Even small problems tip them over into a state of depression. As far as possible, such activities should be avoided due to the effect they have on us. There are much more fulfilling ways to unwind.

HOW TO USE THE MATRIX

Let us now take a look again at quadrant 2, the one that is most effective for long-term growth. By placing tasks in this important but not urgent sphere, we can begin planning for them and lay the foundation for achieving our goals. When these plans are ready, the tasks that ultimately end up in quadrant 1 are automatically reduced, and we no longer have to worry about being firefighting managers. Things will flow naturally towards our goals.

Say for example you have a big interview to prepare for that is to take place in two weeks' time in a distant city. To ensure that you are fully prepared, you have to plan well. You have to prepare a list of tasks that have to be addressed for everything to go smoothly. That list might look like this:

1. Allocate time for thorough preparation
2. Book your flight tickets
3. Reserve a hotel room
4. Arrange conveyance to the interview location
5. Print a copy of your resumé

6. Make copies of your certificates and other credentials
7. Determine your outfit, shop if required
8. Log the contact information of all important parties

As of now, two weeks before the interview, these tasks sit in the second quadrant, important but not urgent. They are to be tended to methodically in reasonable doses as the big day approaches. Doing so will save you from worrying about last-minute anxieties throwing you off on the day of the interview. Make sure you land a full day in advance of the interview, settle in comfortably and review your materials. After a good night's rest, head out early to familiarize yourself with the venue. Then, when the time comes, you'll be as prepared and comfortable as you can be. By thus putting yourself in a position to succeed well ahead of time, you can begin to move steadily towards your desired result. When there is proper planning, execution is a cinch.

The alternative scenario is that we know ahead of time about an upcoming interview but, due to other important and urgent tasks, we neglect our preparation. If this were the case, then all the tasks listed above would go into quadrant 1: important and urgent. All our time would need to be dedicated to these tasks alone, to the exclusion of all the tasks in the other three quadrants. But even if we were able to run through all the tasks before the interview, a single unforeseen problem could still throw everything into irreparable disarray. Our preparation for the interview would be compromised, causing us to appear less confident. What if we ran into a very long line at the car rental kiosk and lost the time we thought we'd have to get freshened up? Being forced to rush to the venue, we'd find ourselves in a panicked state, unsure if we were in the right place. All these stresses would undoubtedly build up and suck the life out of what could have been a much stronger interview. Such is the importance of the second quadrant. By properly managing our long-term tasks, we can bring success within our grasp.

THE TIME MANAGEMENT FORMULA

Our basic strategy for approaching each quadrant can be summed up in the following points:

- Increase the number of tasks in quadrant 2 by planning ahead.
- Reduce the number of tasks in quadrant 1 by consistently executing those in quadrant 2.

- Delegate the tasks placed in quadrant 3 to others where possible.
- Replace any junk activities found in quadrant 4 with more edifying ones, such as reading, nature walks, stimulating talks and the like.

The way to cut down on our quadrant 1 activities is to finish the tasks in quadrant 2 on time. Don't postpone them. If your time is properly allocated, steady progress towards the achievement of your long-term goals is assured.

Quadrant 3 is full of time-sensitive but ultimately unimportant things. Try to reduce the time spent replying to messages and delegate what correspondence you can to others.

Quadrant 4 is typically the junk drawer. Activities that are neither time-sensitive nor important to our overall growth as a person should be trashed. It is better to either engage in more beneficial forms of relaxation or to take care of the tasks we've placed in the more important quadrants.

1.6. TRANSCENDING TWENTY-FIRST CENTURY THREE-DIMENSIONAL MATRIX OF TIME MANAGEMENT

Many productive people are aware of the four quadrants and may even be experts at using them

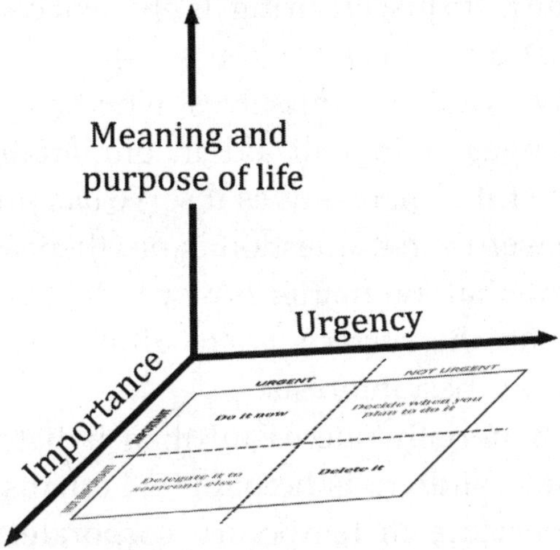

but, despite their heightened productivity, remain unsatisfied.

The fact is that life is about more than numbers. In this world of exponential technological growth, it is easy to get lost in life's peripheral engagements without ever considering what lies within. Even the most successful people tend to fall into bouts of despondence and depression.

This dilemma indicates the need for another dimension in our lives: a spiritual purpose. Having such a purpose frees us up to unlock life's full potential and experience complete satisfaction. Let us now consider how to practically apply this principle to our day-to-day lives.

Aside from just ensuring its efficient completion, we must also check for the substance of a given task. We can ask ourselves whether the work we're engaged in will aid in our attainment of ultimate fulfillment—does it serve *our* purpose? If the answer to that question is no, then we should conclude that, no matter how productive we may appear on the surface, we're ultimately working against our best interests.

If a materially successful man is hated by his wife and children, is he happy? Perhaps he finds some pleasure in temporary corporate victories, but as he comes to terms with the negative impacts he's had on his dependents, do you think those raises will outweigh his guilt at failing the ones closest to him? We cannot measure our life's value in terms of money, power and position (MPP).

- MPP cannot solve relationship problems.
- MPP cannot repair broken relationships.
- MPP cannot replenish lost health.
- MPP cannot provide inner fulfillment on its own.

Though these facts are self-evident, people still spend much of their lives simply trying to accumulate MPP, never realizing the importance of the subtler things until it's too late. In this way, people live as if they'll never die and die having never truly lived at all.

This principle reminds me of the address Steve Jobs delivered to the graduating students at Stanford University on 12 June 2005:

> If you live each day as if it were your last, some day you will be certainly right. Past thirty-three years I have looked in the mirror, I asked myself, if today were the last day of my life, would I want to do what I am about to do today? Whenever the answer has been 'no', I know I need to change. Remembering that we will all be dead soon is the most important tool I have encountered to help me make big choices in my life. Almost everything, all external expectations, all pride, all fear of embarrassment of failure, all these things fall way in the face of death, leaving only what is truly important. Remembering that you are going to die is the best way I know to avoid the trap of thinking you have something to lose. There is no reason not to follow your heart.[2]

2 '"You've got to find what you love," Jobs says', Stanford News, 12 June 2005, https://news.stanford.edu/2005/06/12/youve-got-find-love-jobs-says/#:~:text=This%20is%20a%20prepared%20text,%2C%20on%20June%2012%2C%202005

I completely agree with him. In fact, as I set out writing this book, I became infected with COVID-19, the virus that had by that time already claimed millions of lives around the world. My body was raging with a fever that refused to subside despite ongoing medical treatments. Teetering on the line between life and death, I found that all of my worries and concerns about my various duties in the world became wholly insignificant. The only thing that ran through my mind then was, 'I wish I had better prepared myself for this moment spiritually, I wish I had dedicated more time to selflessly serving others and mastering meditation.'

The fact is, when we are faced with death, all the money and fame in the world become utterly worthless. The only thing that matters then is the degree of integrity with which you lived your life and the amount of time you have dedicated to the world within. Famous actor and comedian Jim Carrey once said, 'I think everybody should get rich and famous and do everything they ever dreamed of so they can see that it's not the answer.'[3]

3 Leonard Kim 'I Think Everyone Should Get Rich and Famous', Medium.com, 3 July 2015, https://medium.com/@mrleonardkim/what-did-jim-carrey-actually-mean-ff98cea4b917

1.7. LASTING HAPPINESS

Happiness is not a car or a bank balance, but a state of consciousness. It cannot be bought at the store; it must be cultivated over time. We cultivate this inner fulfillment by engaging in activities that nourish our hearts and lift our spirits. Such activities, even if great in number, will never bog us down like other activities might. Even before tax incentives came into play, rich men were giving large portions of their hard-earned wealth to charities. Why? Because the act of giving selflessly provides immense satisfaction and fulfillment.

Performing charitable acts, volunteering and engaging in spiritual practices give us immense genuine happiness. Though at first we may be hesitant, after engaging in such activities, we never consider them to have been a waste of time.

The foremost of these fulfilling engagements is the direct cultivation of one's own spirituality. Activities focused on this cleanse the heart of all misgivings and provide one with a beautiful sense of peace and clarity. This good feeling never wanes. Whereas materialistic pursuits may appear at first to be enticing challenges only to eventually lose their spark, spiritual pursuits remain ever fresh, lending themselves unfailingly to newer and more powerful levels of joy and satisfaction.

Consider Winston Churchill's last words in this regard. Churchill is regarded as one of the foremost leaders of all time, someone who rose through the ranks with vigour, always meeting fresh challenges head-on. Even this man, who was so lauded for his accomplishments and success, declared at the end, 'I am bored with it all.'[4]

There is no need for us to live a life of trial and error as so many notable personalities before us have done. Instead, we can learn from their examples and embrace the nature of life in this world, a world in which money, power and position are all ultimately shallow and boring pursuits. Inner fulfillment is decidedly the real test of success.

This being the case, we may consider our tasks and sort them based not only on their urgency and importance but also on the fulfillment they provide us with. The next time you are considering taking up a task, ask yourself the questions, 'Is this going to ultimately contribute to the fulfillment and meaning I want in my life? Can I guarantee that this will not further ruin the earth and nature? Will

---

4 'Churchill's Last Words: "I Am Bored with It All"', *The New York Times*, 2 February 1965, https://www.nytimes.com/1965/02/02/archives/churchills-last-words-i-am-bored-with-it-all.html

this be beneficial to society?' By making a habit of qualifying your activities with these questions, you will ensure that your life becomes one of deep meaning and unwavering contentment. It is at this point that you will be able to truly call yourself successful.

We have now learned how to sort tasks according to their urgency and *true* importance so as to divide our time in the most efficient and effective manner. This, however, is just the beginning of truly mastering the art of time management. To most effectively turn our plans into reality and simultaneously achieve inner fulfillment, we need to go one step further in effective time management.

1.8. TIME MANAGEMENT: ONE STEP FURTHER

According to the yoga wisdom texts, to take birth as a human out of the millions of other life-forms on Earth is very rare and coveted. It is also surmised that we don't have much of a say in the matter. After all, none of us knew which country we'd be born in or who our parents would be. It was not our choice to come to this particular planet at this particular time. Our parents didn't arrange for the minute details of our appearance; they simply acted on a desire to have a child, and we appeared. If we consider these questions deeply, we will eventually come to more mystical considerations.

The yoga wisdom texts contend that we are spiritual beings full of happiness. However, being encased in a material body and further encased by the material world, we, though spiritual by nature, end up experiencing life and the world materially. Due to our prolonged association with matter, we misidentify with our material body and forget about our essential spiritual identity. Mistakenly identifying with the body, we exploit it for sensory pleasure instead of recognizing the intrinsic bliss within.

As long as our mind identifies with the body, we are constantly pulled in different directions in pursuit of external pleasures. We do derive some enjoyment from this yanking, but can a slave ever be truly happy? As long as our mind and senses are bossing us around, we'll always feel a sense of lack, no matter how much pleasure we accrue. In this way, our dastardly mind becomes our worst enemy, always plotting our perpetual dissatisfaction. By instead controlling the mind and using it for truly pleasurable ends, we can make it our best friend. Instead of tricking us into situations that only prolong our despondence, the mind instead discerns between that which brings lasting happiness and the bait-and-switch scam of hollow material enjoyment.

The author of the ancient Yoga Sutras, Patanjali, said that to control the mind is the true definition of yoga or inner fulfillment.[5] Another ancient text, the Bhagavad Gita, compares the pull of the senses to wild horses dragging us in different directions. However, if the charioteer (our intelligence) grasps the reins (our mind) tightly and guides the chariot towards more savoury destinations, directed by values instead of the pursuit of pleasure, then one can find genuine happiness. We should align our goals with our vision of ultimate happiness. To instead base them on short-term pleasures yields only wild discontent. True happiness and, indeed, true success come from discipline employed for a higher cause, a deeper cause, one that starts within.

There is a beautiful story in this regard about the ancient King Sibi in the Bhagavata Purana. Sibi was an extremely kind and generous king. One day, while he was lounging in his palace with a few courtiers, a dove flew into his lap and began begging him for protection. The king, being a righteous ruler, would never refuse protection to any of his faithful subjects. He agreed to shelter the bird.

5 'What would Patanjali say about our changing states of mind?', Yogapedia.com, https://www.yogapedia.com/7/9172/self/ego/what-would-patanjali-say-about-our-changing-states-of-mind

Suddenly, a hawk that had been in hot pursuit of the dove appeared. Distraught with hunger, the hawk politely asked the king to release the dove.

The king refused, telling the hawk that he had given his word to protect the dove.

'I am also your subject,' the hawk retorted. 'I need food to maintain my family!'

The king then offered the hawk various vegetarian options. Uninterested, the hawk squawked, 'I am *starving*, as is my family. If we don't get a proper meal soon, we will surely perish.' After earnestly pondering the dilemma for some time, the king decided not to sacrifice any of his subjects but to offer the hawk flesh from his own body. The hawk desperately demanded an amount of flesh equal to the weight of the dove. The king, undeterred, called for a scale and began filling one side with his very self while the dove trembled upon the other.

Mystically, no matter how much flesh he added to the scale, it would not balance out. Finally, amidst the cries of his horrified courtiers, the king sat upon the scale, offering his entire self to the hawk in an effort to do the right thing for both of his dependent subjects. At this moment, both the dove and the hawk revealed their true forms as celestial beings who had come down to test the king's qualities of compassion and honour. Having received evidence of his unwavering selflessness even in the direst of circumstances, they blessed him with a long, healthy and prosperous life. This story shows us that true success and true happiness come from selfless service. They cannot be found in temporary positions or possessions or circumstances in this world.

1.9. LIFE'S TRIANGLE

Try thinking of your life as a triangle, with its three corners representing your work life, interpersonal life and spiritual life respectively.

- **Work life:** We must work to earn the money required to take care of our body, our family, our home and our possessions.

- **Interpersonal life:** Simply eating and surviving is not enough. In order to feel some sense of fulfillment, we must have intimate relations with friends and family. The human is a social being. Loneliness breeds despair.
- **Spiritual life:** In essence, we are spiritual beings. We simply inhabit and operate a material body. To feel completely fulfilled, we must cater to our intrinsic nature. Though the most neglected, this corner of the triangle is the most essential. If taken care of, it enhances our work and interpersonal dealings. You may be surprised to know that some of the world's most successful people, like Apple's Steve Jobs and Virgin's Richard Branson, considered themselves avid spiritual practitioners.

One may wonder whether there is something about spirituality that gives practitioners an overall edge. The fact is that we will all go through trying times in life. Even Steve Jobs was fired from his own company at one point. What makes the difference, however, is the way we respond to these adversities. When spiritual people face difficulties, instead of becoming overwhelmed by their external circumstances, they look within. Understanding both their connection to a higher power and their identity as wholly separate from their distressing circumstances, they are able to step back, objectively assess the situation and begin working towards a solution. In this way, they methodically but dispassionately climb their way back up from wherever they may have fallen to. If more people understood the value of spirituality, especially in overcoming inevitable difficulties, perhaps the twelfth-most common cause of death in the U.S. would be something other than suicide.[6]

The ancient wisdom texts provide us with the example of the clay ball versus the rubber one. Both may be dropped from the same place, and both immediately begin plummeting towards the earth below. The difference comes when they hit rock bottom. While the rubber ball (the spiritualist) absorbs the impact, embracing its fate as an opportunity to learn and ultimately bouncing back higher, the clay ball, unable to accept and own its circumstances, shatters.

At the end of the day, life is a winding highway. It is full of twists and turns. This is true of every life, regardless of the influence of wealth or status. Cultivating spiritual qualities such as humility,

---

6 'Transforming the understanding and treatment of mental illnesses', National Institute of Mental Health, https://www.nimh.nih.gov/health/statistics/suicide

patience and tolerance allows us to be able to face those unexpected turns with poise and weather the occasional storm as we progress towards our ultimate destination.

SUMMARY

Eisenhower Decision Matrix

1. Increase the activities of quadrant 2 (important but not urgent) by planning well in advance.
2. Reduce the activities of quadrant 1 (important and urgent) by getting things done on time.
3. Delegate the activities of quadrant 3 (urgent but not important).
4. Eliminate the activities of quadrant 4 (not important, not urgent).

Twenty-first Century Three-dimensional Matrix of Time Management

- Increase the activities that give you a sense of fulfillment.
- Adjust or eliminate the activities that leave you feeling unfulfilled.

- Find a sweet spot where your goals align perfectly with your values.
- Strike a balance between your work, interpersonal and spiritual lives, always giving special emphasis to the spiritual.

EXERCISES

1. Compile a list of your values.
2. Define your short and long-term goals along with the timelines in which you hope to achieve them.
3. Draw out your weekly schedule within the four quadrants: Do (Quadrant 1), Decide (Quadrant 2), Delegate (Quadrant 3) and Delete (Quadrant 4).
4. Once you have divided your tasks according to importance and urgency, organize them for the day in a chronological sequence.

CHAPTER 2

The Obstacles Ahead

2.1. NEW YEAR'S DISSOLUTIONS

Why is time management important?

Yahoo News reports that some 80 per cent of New Year's resolutions are abandoned by February of the same year.[7] The most common New Year's resolution is to lose weight. Perhaps second on that list is to learn something new. But, considering our conviction on New Year's Eve, why don't we ever seem to keep track of these goals?

The fact is, on New Year's Eve, we generally make resolutions emotionally. Most people don't take that next step to practically plan how to

---

7 Joseph Luciani, 'Why 80% of New Year's Resolutions Fail', *Yahoo News*.

achieve their goals. Success demands a practical plan, and that means responsibly allocating time and energy on a daily basis to working towards our goals and monitoring our progress. If we detect a gap, we must fill that gap with extra time and effort so as to stay on track.

We may be enthused to make a schedule, but a strong sense of discipline is required to stick to it. Otherwise, our dreams will remain only dreams.

Being a spiritual coach, I tailor plans for people who have realized the value of spirituality in their work and family lives. I suggest small adjustments to their lifestyle to enable them to realize the immense intrinsic wealth derived from the yoga process. Those enthused to reap such benefits employ discipline and experience the results. Others, who shy away from such discipline, give up, even if they have understood the treasures they stand to gain.

The moral of the above story is that success in any field demands discipline. Otherwise, our aspirations will simply float around in our minds, never actually materializing. We will go on thinking, 'One day I will become this. One day I will become that.' But that day will never come. So, the question then is, what can we practically do to make our dreams a reality?

2.2. WHERE DID THE TIME GO?

Sometimes, we want to finish a task or a project by a certain date and time but fail to do so. This generally tends to happen for a few reasons. Let us take a deeper look at some of the obstacles that can get in our way and see how we can navigate around them to keep moving forward.

Too Much on Our Plate

Out of enthusiasm, we accept so many tasks that, unknowingly, we start underperforming. While we work hard on one important task, others start slipping through the cracks. Immersed in our work, we finally look at the clock and are baffled by the realization that the whole day has passed by while other pressing matters have been left unattended. Now is the time to reassess our schedule and the allocation of time to tasks therein. This analysis will sometimes indicate the necessity of a self-assessment as well. After all, many of us need to learn when to politely say 'no' to new engagements. One time, I asked a senior monk to deliver an important seminar. He sincerely thanked me for the invitation, but politely refused my request, saying, 'I am fully occupied.'

Too Tied Up

Consider the fact that our time, our energy and our capacity to act are all limited while our aspirations are endless. Because of this conflict, we often find ourselves tangled up in more responsibilities than we can handle. As a result, we see our time, energy and capacity become even more limited and our activities become stifled. It is better to overachieve in a few tasks than to generally underperform in an effort to accomplish many. This overloading pulls too many tasks into the 'urgent and important' quadrant, leaving us in a state of constant flux as our efficiency and effectiveness nosedive. Just as a magnifying glass focuses a beam of light onto an object and produces fire, when we fully focus on a controlled number of tasks, our full power can be realized.

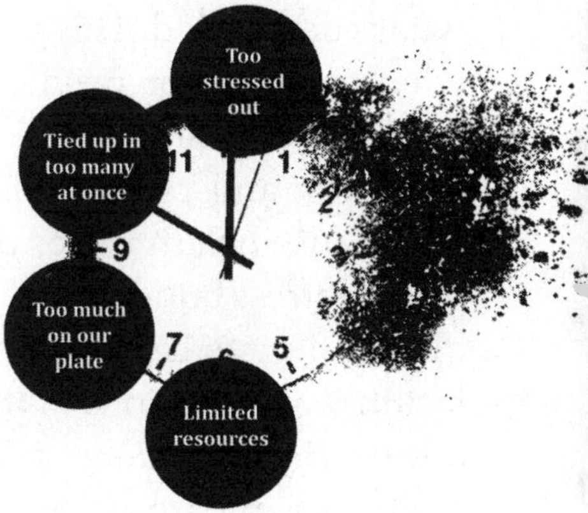

Too Stressed Out

Due to inevitable changes in one's personal or professional life, it is natural to become stressed out from time to time. Most often, we can boil down the cause of stress to our resources falling short of what's demanded. This gap in what we have versus what we want or need creates a kind of tension that's hard to shake. This tension reverberates in our work and personal lives and, if ignored, can even cause health issues down the road. When we feel the stress building up, it is extremely important to take time to centre ourselves and recognize the fact that all situations in this world, no matter how devastating, produce only temporary reactions. All things must pass. By taking the time to centre yourself, you keep from letting yourself be bogged down by a negative attitude and set yourself up for success in the long run.

We need additional resources. We may, on many occasions, feel mentally prepared to deal with a challenge or a situation but find that the forces around us are in some way lacking. Interestingly, this problem often arises as a result of growth. As a person, company or community grows, it is but natural that more resources are required to meet their increasing needs and sustain their upward momentum. One should be mindful in such cases of the needs of the entity that one is responsible for and take necessary measures to ensure it is or they are supported. On the negative side, a lack of organization within any kind of project leads to a kind of hole in the boat, through which both human potential and resources flow out and are wasted, as a result of which the ship gradually begins to sink. In such cases, one must diligently design and implement a suitable system to ensure that these holes in the boat are plugged and similar fissures never appear again.

Obviously, the solutions to all these problems are 'easier said than done'. So, one may wonder, what is required to actually solve the problems that hold us back? Let us take a deeper look at the keys to steady growth.

2.3. FOOTPRINTS IN THE SAND

> *You can't make footprints in the sands of time by sitting down.*
>
> —Bob Moawad

Laziness is the #1 dream-killer known to man. Many people aspire to achieve great things but very few people take the steps necessary to do so. In order to actually turn our dreams into reality, we must create plans of action and stick to them. Otherwise, all our dreams will remain dreams.

As human beings, we are endowed with a special degree of free will. Our capacity to think critically and act is thousands of times more developed than that of other living beings on the planet. Despite our heightened abilities, we are often stifled by one especially formidable enemy: laziness. Laziness convinces us that we'll be happier if we just take it easy, but, in reality, we find ourselves feeling more and more despondent as the gap between what we aspire to be and what we are grows.

The great 16th-century yogi and saint Rupa Goswami listed three weapons that were effective in combating this terrible enemy: enthusiasm, determination and patience.[8]

Enthusiasm

Rupa Goswami defined enthusiasm as steadily endeavouring with intelligence. If we endeavour blindly without proper forethought, then failures will consume us both in volume and emotional impact. But, if we meet all challenges with intelligence and actively figure out how to fix the problems at hand, we can continue our forward progress over unlimited bumps in the road. In

8 Rupa Gosvami, *The Nectar of Instruction*

this way, enthusiasm also means action. First, we assess a situation, and then we take the necessary action to rectify whatever is wrong with it. Winston Churchill once said, 'Success consists of going from failure to failure without loss of enthusiasm.'

In the 1920s, a journalist asked Thomas Edison how it felt to fail 1000 times in his attempt to invent the incandescent lightbulb. He replied, 'I didn't fail 1000 times. **The lightbulb was an invention with 1000 steps**.' By cultivating in ourselves such a mentality, we can ensure that we remain enthusiastic no matter how many 'steps' it takes to reach our ultimate goals.

Determination

We can think of determination as the fuel that pushes us toward our goals. With determination comes the resolve required to keep pushing ahead no matter what we face. However, the ancient wisdom texts tell us of three different gradations of determination that we should be mindful of. Let us consider these three categories of determination and figure out which can be most helpful to us:

Sattva

The best kind of determination is sattvic (in the 'mode of goodness'). From this mode is born a

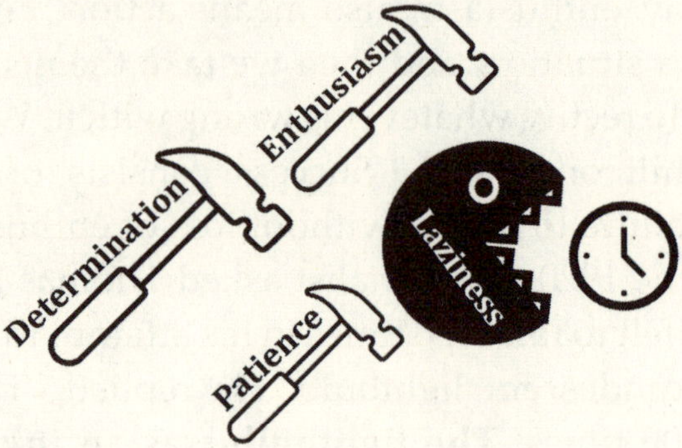

lasting push based on internal strength. Those who control the urges of the mind and senses naturally possess this energy. An example of this from the ancient yogic wisdom texts is that of Vibhishan from the Ramayana. He was the brother of Ravana, who was the king of Lanka, an island in the Indian ocean. Vibhishan always led a clean and virtuous life. Being possessed of sattva, he always made the right choices. When his brother Ravana abducted Sita (Lord Rama's wife) Vibhishan disapproved. He predicted that this action would cause the ruination of the whole royal family. Vibhishan suggested that Ravana return Sita to Lord Rama to avoid war. When Ravana refused to heed his advice and banished him from Lanka, Vibhishan was determined to do what was right and went to Lord Rama. As an ardent follower of Rama, Vibhishan endured countless challenges in his service, but because of his internal strength and selfless motivations, he always prevailed in his duties. Because he was not a slave to his own enjoyment, he was never shaken by any austerities he had to endure. So, that determination which is motivated by selfless desire and strengthened by a steady mind and senses can be considered the most powerful and enduring.

Rajas

The less powerful but more prevalent kind of determination that we see in the world today is born of rajas or 'the mode of passion'. From this energy is born a fleeting determination founded in materialistic desires. When we are motivated purely by selfish desires and are not properly guided by spiritual values, regardless of material advancement, our internal world gets depleted. This kind of determination leads to an inflation of ego, and, as the old adage goes, pride comes before the fall. This determination produces peaks and valleys of both productivity and emotional stability. In the end, no matter how much one has accomplished, internal success will always evade one.

A great example of this kind of determination is Ravana, who was the worst kind of overachiever.

He acquired massive stores of wealth without any consideration of the effect he was having on others. Along with his power and money grew an unshakeable arrogance. As a result of his pride, he began committing many mistakes that would become the seeds of his ultimate downfall. Intoxicated by wealth, he decided to do the unthinkable and kidnap the divine king's wife. As a result, he lost everything that he had worked so hard for and perished.

Tamas

Last on our spectrum comes determination in the 'mode of darkness' or tamas. People who cannot overcome their vices and are determined only to perpetuate the things that hold them back fall in this category. This determination is marred by fear, illusion, misdirected energy and, ultimately, humiliation. People who are possessed of this kind of determination find themselves absorbed in bodily consciousness, motivated by selfish motives that stifle them materially, spiritually and, often, even physically. They harm both themselves and society.

The classic example of this is Kumbakarna, the brother of Ravana. Kumbakarna would sleep for six months at a time and, on awakening, eat unlimited amounts of meat and drink barrels of liquor. To him, life meant eating food, drinking liquor and sleeping. Modern day examples of this are persons who are motivated to do work that harms themselves and others. Such people are aware of the detrimental effects their work has on others and they consciously choose to capitalize on human weakness with seemingly no remorse for the hurt they cause. Such work is the most torturous to one's internal world. Many such people are eventually apprehended by the law for their dastardly work, but even before that, their sense of self-worth is punished severely. Such people, in reality, know only suffering from beginning to end and the lives they live embody that negativity.

Conclusion? Strive for sattva! We will explore in more detail what it means to cultivate sattva in the pages to follow.

Patience

Our last weapon in the war against laziness is patience. Patience is the buffer between something not going our way and our becoming discouraged by it. Patience, though a peaceful emotion, is perhaps the most essential sword in our arsenal.

This is because it sharpens the other two. When we are patient in our endeavours, our determination and enthusiasm are strengthened. Patience grants us the mental stability required to bear all the challenges that come our way with grace and soberly discern the best ways to move forward in their wake. By maintaining our mental equilibrium in this way, we maximize our chances of reaching the ultimate destination, no matter how dicey things get.

***

All of these factors reflect the mentality required to advance towards our goals. By cultivating such a state of mind, we create a solution-oriented and creative space within ourselves. This kind of calm gives way to the innovation required to truly make a difference in the world. The fact is that our present lifestyle will determine our future one. Wasting a few hours in a day may not seem like a huge deal, but all those hours add up over the years. Let us combat the dreaded enemy of laziness with the characteristics mentioned above. In this way, we too may come to realize unmatched and unbounded success.

2.4. 'ONE DAY' OR 'DAY ONE': YOU DECIDE

We all have dreams. What are yours?

Some desire to become the CEO of a company. Others dream of learning to play the guitar. Still others dream of quitting their job and starting their own successful business. Regardless of what the dreams are, for many, these seeds will never fructify. *The most important thing is not the dream itself but what we do to make it happen.* To make a thought a reality, we need to act on it. Nothing materializes without endeavour. This means allocating time and resources to our dream consistently so as to move closer to manifesting it. The fact is that everyone dreams of their ideal life; many even harbour strong desires to achieve it, but very few take on the sacrifices required to make it happen.

The dreamers never make any real endeavours. The desirers may make some efforts, but as soon as they come across difficulties, they give up. But the determined, those willing to do whatever it takes, persevere; they enthusiastically endure any and all difficulties on their path, having already decided that failure is not an option.

Different Kinds of Workers

So, the question naturally arises: how can we make sure we remain in the 'determined' category rather than the other two? For the answer to this query, we can again look at one of the themes in the ancient wisdom texts. Just as there are three different kinds of determination, there are also three different kinds of workers in this world. These workers are also distinguished by the modes we mentioned previously: sattva (goodness), rajas (passion) and tamas (ignorance). All the actions one performs are influenced in some way by these forces of nature. Let us now take a closer look at each of them and the effects they have on an aspiring achiever.

Sattva

> One who performs duty without false ego, with great determination and enthusiasm, is said to be a worker in the mode of goodness.[9]

Those in the mode of sattva act in a calm but methodical manner. They are impelled by their values and sense of duty and so are never overwhelmed by the kind of volatility that may affect others in the course of their work. Such people are experts at sticking to a plan, as their minds are not easily deterred by distractions. Being possessed

9 Bhagavad Gita (18.26)

of self-awareness and knowledge of what brings them true happiness, they are always satisfied and clear-minded. They may pursue their goals in this world but their ultimate goal is spiritual progress leading to self-realization.

Rajas

> The worker who is attached to the results of his work, who desires to enjoy those results, and who is greedy, selfish and motivated by pleasure is said to be in the mode of passion.[10]

Those in the mode of rajas work tirelessly, driven by a strong desire to prove themselves and compete with others. Because of their passionate and emotional mentality, they often make mistakes in the execution of their work, which causes setbacks and delays in the long run. Such people are great at making schedules and getting things started but are often distracted and ultimately deterred by other opportunities. Their tireless pursuit of endless stimuli often leads to burnout. Their ultimate goal is to enjoy the fruits of their labour in the form of money, power, recognition and pleasure.

10 Bhagavad Gita (18.27)

Tamas

> The worker who is always engaged in work against the principles of nature, who is materialistic, obstinate, cheating and expert in insulting others, and who is lazy, always morose and procrastinating is said to be a worker in the mode of ignorance.[11]

Workers in the mode of ignorance can hardly be called workers at all. These are the dreamers who prefer to do the bare minimum in life and hope for the best. Owing to their lazy and misguided mentality, they tend to only move further away from achieving any goals they may have, always making the wrong decisions or refusing to do the work necessary to execute the right ones. Their ultimate goal is to avoid all strain and simply float through life enjoying its most base pleasures. They generally end up destitute and depressed.

CONCLUSION

The most effective mentality with which to work is sattva or the mode of goodness. To maximize our efficiency, we should adopt this mode by cultivating our spiritual life through daily practices like yoga

11 Bhagavad Gita (18.28)

and meditation and adopting a plant-based diet that is devoid of the fear hormones present in animal flesh. Such a lifestyle assures one of access to the mode of goodness, after which the results will speak for themselves.

Over the decades that I've spent living with monks, I've watched many of my peers work tirelessly for the welfare of human society. Despite their zen, they work seven days a week, 365 days a year, without any vacations or any breaks in enthusiasm or determination. I've seen many such souls accomplish great things and even become internationally famous. And I've also watched them remain level-headed through all of it, continuing to perform menial services like scrubbing toilets and mopping floors. These are the happiest men I've come across in my life. Their secret? Sattva!

We may also consider the modes our subordinates are in when gauging how to deal with them. Those in the mode of goodness will not need much outside help. Those in the mode of passion will be driven but will require some occasional guidance to ensure they stay on the right track. Those in ignorance will need constant monitoring to ensure they are performing their duties and not cutting corners. By identifying these modes in ourselves and in others, we can fine-tune our state of being for maximum efficiency and flow.

Each Day Is a Miniature Life

> 'Your days are your life in miniature form. As you live your hours, so you craft your years.'
>
> – Robin Sharma

Whether we like it or not, the clock is ticking. The most powerful destroying force in all existence is this very element: time. Under the pressure of time, mountains become dust, surging rivers dry up and even the most incredibly beautiful among us become old and decrepit. It is no secret that our time in this world is limited. *But*—that doesn't mean time cannot work in our favour.

Through the proper utilization of our time as the years pass by, we become increasingly better-positioned in our lives. This long process starts at the day-to-day level. Just as a house is composed of so many bricks, our lives are composed of so many days. By taking measures to ensure each brick is properly laid, we ensure that the house is sturdy; by ensuring that each day is properly spent to the best of our abilities, we guarantee our own ultimate success.

So, how can we make sure that we are making the *most* of our days? To answer this, we must look within—specifically at our *thoughts*. The

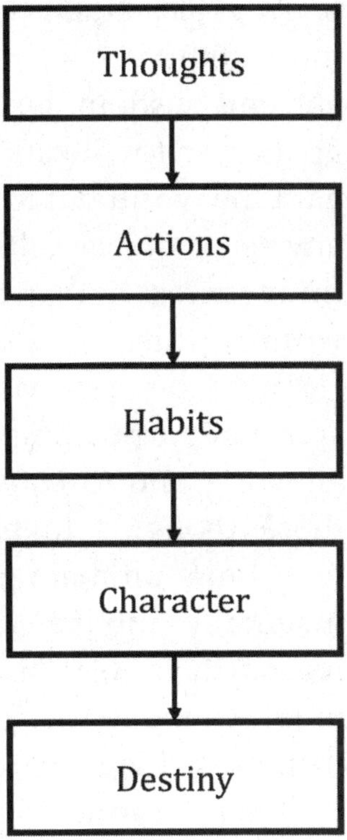

Buddha said, 'The mind is everything; what you think, you become.' This may sound a bit incredible but let us take a closer look at how important our thoughts truly are.

Our actions come from our thoughts. These actions become our habits. These habits determine our character and our character determines our ultimate destination. Take a moment to deeply reflect on this sequence:

From thoughts come actions.

From actions come habits.

Our habits define our character.

Our character determines our destiny.

So, from this one may logically conclude that our ultimate destination in life is determined by our thoughts. The question then becomes: *how can I fine-tune my thoughts so as to reach my desired destination*? This of course will depend on what one's goal actually is. For those who desire the most complete form of success in this life, the ancient wisdom texts recommend the ultimate goal of self-realization. While a materialist may gain the world but lose their soul and, resultantly, any sense of *true* fulfillment, the spiritual warrior finds success both in the material world and in the world within.

The sober resolve that comes with having a spiritual purpose imparts clarity to one's thoughts, allowing one to consciously monitor and adjust those thoughts to ensure they remain aligned with one's ultimate goal. On the other hand, the materially motivated are ever-disturbed. They regard their work as the be-all and end-all, due to which the issues that inevitably arise debilitate them, wrecking whatever mental equilibrium they may have formerly achieved. This weakness of mind that results from a weak objective puts them at a considerable disadvantage compared to their more enlightened counterparts.

The mental fortitude of an enlightened worker certainly goes a long way. But it is not all that is required to achieve success. On a more practical level, one must ensure that their *planning* is pristine. Let's take a deeper look at the importance of a good plan.

Failure to Plan = Planning to Fail

By failing to prepare, you are preparing to fail.
—Benjamin Franklin

Everyone wants to win. What separates the winners from the rest is the quality of their plan and execution. Bad planning leads to ambiguity, wasted time and, ultimately, poor performance. Good planning, on the other hand, is clear and specific. It is a result of in-depth analysis, not whimsy and assumptions. It also involves taking into account all that could go wrong and ensuring one's readiness to respond to those scenarios.

A standardized and in-depth way of fortifying one's plan is to use the SWOT analysis, wherein one identifies one's strengths, weaknesses, opportunities and threats in the context of pursuing a certain goal. Taking it a step further, one should not just identify these different elements but also understand how one's threats may be transformed into opportunities. In a similar way, one should determine how to bolster oneself in such a way that one's weaknesses may ultimately be transformed into strengths. By strengthening oneself in this way, one can use one's plan as a sturdy bridge upon which to confidently march towards the ultimate destination.

To further illustrate the power of planning, let us look at the contrasting cases of two men who led parallel expeditions to the South Pole.

In 1911, Roald Amundsen and Robert Scott[12] both set out on a race to be the first to reach the South Pole. Both men were seasoned skippers acclaimed for their maritime accomplishments. However, while their accolades and abilities were similar, their fates were not. Amundsen and his crew of nineteen reached the South Pole in an unprecedented thirty-four days and returned safely without losing a single man. Scott, on the other hand, perished alongside his entire crew shortly after arriving in Antarctica. How did the efforts of these two men of apparently equal measure produce such different results? The key was in the planning.

The average temperature in the South Pole during the summer is -18°F. Upon reaching the coast of Antarctica, both explorers were required to travel hundreds of miles to reach the pole. Amundsen had taken extreme precautions for the extreme conditions that lay ahead. He lived for

12 'Comparison of the Amundsen and Scott expeditions', Wikipedia, https://en.wikipedia.org/wiki/Comparison_of_the_Amundsen_and_Scott_expeditions

some time with the natives of northern Canada, closely studying their ways of survival in tundra-like conditions. He picked up what would prove to be invaluable insights, like the fact that certain dog breeds survive the snow better than any other hauling animal. He also learned to move slowly in arctic conditions, as any sweat is liable to freeze and cause hypothermia. For three years before setting out, he and his team maintained a rigorous fitness regimen that would grant them the stamina to push forward when the going got tough.

On the other hand, Scott, despite his personal capabilities, failed to adequately plan and suffered the consequences. Instead of huskies, Scott opted for ponies and a motor sledge; the former died and the latter stopped functioning after a short stint in the tundra. As a result, the men themselves had to lug their supplies, which exhausted and slowed them to a deadly degree. On top of this, the provisions Scott had brought along for his crew were also inadequate. Whereas Amundsen brought three tons of supplies for five men, Scott brought only one ton for seventeen. Whereas Amundsen brought four thermometers to monitor the conditions, Scott brought only one, which broke. Even though both parties had left at the same time, when Amundsen reached the pole, Scott and his men were 360 miles behind, miserably dragging their once pony-drawn sledges and sweating profusely.

By the time Scott and his four surviving men finally reached the South Pole, Amundsen and his entire crew were almost back at the coast, ready to sail home to Norway. While Scott and his survivors were finally wiped out by lack of provisions and fatigue, Amundsen was declared a hero. Upon even the most surface-level analysis, it is clear that planning made all the difference. And what a difference it was.

No matter how skilled and determined one may be, a failure to plan can ruin it all. We should never sacrifice planning for passion thinking the latter to be sufficient. A failure to plan is a plan to fail.

2.5. POISON AT FIRST, NECTAR IN THE END

Changing our lifestyle in an effort to grow as human beings does not come without its fair share of strain. After all, we are conditioned to think and act in certain ways according to our upbringing and experiences. To break free of this mould will always require a special effort. Breaking bad habits and replacing them with positive ones can feel like ingesting poison at first, but, in the end, those new healthy habits will turn to nectar.

As we work towards this nectarine end goal, there will be difficult times. Our newfound lifestyle may require ending close relationships with people who want to hold us back. We may commit myriad mistakes, stumbling again and again in our attempts to walk freely. But we should always remember that the night is darkest just before the dawn. Those dark times are the ones in which we must ramp up our patience and determination. By overcoming those adverse times, we gain renewed vigour and self-belief. This is the process by which the bitterness of hardship is slowly transformed into the sweetness of success.

The Illusion of Failure

Success is but the tip of the iceberg. Beneath the surface of most success stories, one will find countless hours of hard work, countless obstacles that were overcome and the perseverance, patience and enthusiasm to push through it all. Many people think that success starts and ends with the tip they see; they give up as soon as they encounter a challenge. Only very few possess the qualities required to push through all the ice-water that surrounds their initial endeavours. Those who *do* have what it takes become great individuals; some even change the world. In this connection, let us reflect on one such pioneer whose determination in the face of adversity helped shape the world as we know it today.

Thomas Edison was determined to change the world with electricity by engineering the world's very first electric lightbulb.[13] For years, he and his associates developed and experimented with over 3,000 different ideas for the first bulb. It was an incredible endeavour. Most others would have surely given up after the first dozen failures. But as we know, to bring about change is difficult—it is like poison at first.

Finally, Edison found that, in a vacuumed environment, an incandescent lamp can produce light by way of a heated filament. This discovery, however, was nowhere near the end of his journey. To make a vacuum-sealed bulb in the 19th century was unheard of. He would have to somehow

13 Edison's Lightbulb, The Franklin Institute, https://www.fi.edu/en/history-resources/edisons-lightbulb#:~:text=Edison%20decided%20to%20try%20a,and%20longer%20with%20each%20test

produce the first one. Once he and his men were able to do so, he then had to procure a filament that would glow for an extended period of time without requiring an unreasonable amount of electric power. This was akin to searching for a needle in a haystack; the filament could be produced from countless materials, but the exact right one had to be found.

In 1879, he experimented with a platinum filament. While it did glow efficiently, it only lasted a few hours. 'Tungsten would be perfect,' he thought, but, at the time, the kind of technology that would be required to produce such extremely thin tungsten filaments was decades away. He would go on to experiment with thousands of other metals to no avail. Determined, he decided to try plant materials. This led to an even more strenuous endeavour, as he tried to secure different plant fibres from all over the world in search of the perfect one. Finally, he found it. After endless struggles and failures, he carbonized a bamboo filament which could burn for more than 1,200 hours. With the grandest sense of triumph imaginable, Edison secured the patent.

'Before I got through,' he recalled, 'I tested no fewer than 6,000 vegetable growths, and ransacked the world for the most suitable filament material.

'The electric light has caused me the greatest amount of study and has required the most elaborate experiments; I was never myself discouraged or inclined to be hopeless of success. I cannot say the same for all my associates.'

It was Edison's determination in the face of unprecedented apparent failures and strain that empowered him to change the world. Upon finally securing the patent and refining the bulb, he started the world's first city-wide power grid in New York City and lit up the atmosphere in which countless other men and women hungry for success would attempt to reach similar heights. Undoubtedly, many will try, but without the strength to endure the poison of adversity, the nectar of victory will always remain just out of reach.

SUMMARY

- Enthusiasm, determination and patience are prerequisites to success.
- Meticulous planning makes all the difference. If we fail to plan, we plan to fail.
- Genius is one percent inspiration and ninety-nine percent *perspiration*.
- Schedule your tasks and execute them with discipline.
- Sattva-based activity breeds good results.

- One must work hard, enduring the poison of strain to taste the nectar of success.

QUESTIONS

1. Have you ever experienced a delay in a project? What caused it?

____

____

____

____

2. Which of the desirable qualities discussed in this chapter do you possess?

____

____

____

____

3. Which of the desirable qualities discussed in this chapter would you like to cultivate?

____

____

____

____

CHAPTER 3

Obstacles in Time Management

Despite our desire to efficiently manage our time, there are many internal enemies that will try to stop us from doing so. We very soon realize that time management is about not merely curating a to-do list and checking off the boxes but actually disciplining ourselves to ensure we get the most done that we can in an efficient and effective manner. Let us take a look at some of the many obstacles that keep us from realizing our full time management potential and how we may snuff them out. The culprits are as follows:

1. Fear of missing out (FOMO)
2. Lack of self-belief
3. Indulging the urge to waste time
4. Poor time allocation

5. Poor prioritization
6. Over-extending
7. Rising late
8. Procrastination
9. Multi-tasking
10. Scrolling for relaxation

3.1. FEAR OF MISSING OUT (FOMO)

Due to social media, FOMO has become the second-most widespread epidemic of the 21st century. Did you check your social media messages today? Did you see who posted what? Did you know some of your friends went on a cruise together and are having a fantastic time? Your colleague just posted a picture of his shiny new sportscar. Did you see your ex-girlfriend partying it up in Vegas with her new beau? Your cousin just got accepted to Columbia Law School and is moving to NYC! Your childhood friend just landed a big job at Google—amazing!

'Everyone is doing so great! They're all enjoying life so much! But what about me? Am I the only one missing out?' Can you relate to these thoughts? If so, you have experienced FOMO.

Don't worry, these days it's near impossible to avoid it. In today's world of information overload, with millions of people sharing their best experiences with the world (and leaving out the rest), you are bound to feel a bit dejected. By letting our minds latch onto the illusory worlds people create, we end up becoming hyper-dissatisfied with our own life. If you're able to put down your phone and turn on the TV instead, you'll be bombarded with advertisements for products and experiences that you're told will make you happy—the FOMO persists! Finally, convinced that you need something to make you feel better, you go back to your phone and scroll for endless hours, searching for a satisfaction that never comes. In your mind's manic search for something fulfilling, that sense of fulfillment only drifts further and further away.

FOMO is not just a catchy term but a serious force that can stifle our progressive march towards our ultimate happiness. So, how do we overcome this formidable adversary?

Recognize the False Hype of Temporary, Artificial Happiness

All images of materialistic pleasures represent an ephemeral, insubstantial kind of happiness. First, we must understand that happiness is not to be found in a person or a thing but in a state of consciousness. This is why you'll find dirt-poor people who are spiritually-minded and exude happiness at all times, whereas many of the richest, most powerful men in the world are miserable to the point where they are unable to sleep at night and require psychiatric medication to make it through. If we simply follow our mind and senses instead of our heart, we'll be pulled into a perpetually-unsatisfied state; after all, the mind's cravings are *endless*. But, if we cultivate inner peace based on discipline and a divine connection, we might find the true happiness for which everyone searches.

Find Happiness in the Little Things

I remember being struck, while paying a visit to a spiritually-minded American man, by the various beautiful, ornate, intricately carved wood designs in his home. Upon learning that the man had made them all himself, I asked how he had done so.

'Everything is on the internet,' he replied.

I was amazed—not just at the beauty of his designs but also at his decision to dedicate his time and effort to such simple yet profound work. Sometimes, happiness can be found in the little things.

Our FOMO prevents such little things from occurring to us as potential avenues for fulfillment. By constantly thinking about what others have or what others are doing, we miss out on the simple beauty of what we have within and before us. We miss the beauty of nature that we have access to: the warmth in the rays of sunlight that enter our windows, the rainbow after the rain, the earth's aroma after a refreshing summer downpour. What is stopping us from entering the woods and meditating on the exquisite stillness of a pond, on the unique beauty of a flower, on the lovely scenes naturally present in creation? Though at first such experiences may feel ordinary, I can assure you that the happiness they provide is enough to cure any amount of FOMO produced by witnessing the pseudo-happiness advertised by others.

Learn to Appreciate

Before we try to add something new to our life, we should first learn to appreciate what we already have. Think of the simple things first. Can you imagine life without water or air? Without the sun's rays or the honeybee's hard work? Take a moment to appreciate the arrangements God has made here on Earth for us to experience the beauty of life. It is important to appreciate all the good things that have happened to us. We can even appreciate the adversities sent our way as opportunities to develop our resilience. Finally, we can appreciate ourselves and the desire we all carry to evolve as human beings. As a result of this kind of appreciation, we may find that we are already complete in and of ourselves. Perhaps that thing we thought we needed isn't so necessary anymore.

Find Happiness in Service

Real happiness comes not from receiving things but from giving to others. Real happiness lies in service. This is because to love (which ultimately means to serve) is the nature of the soul. If we look around, we'll notice that everyone and everything is serving in some way. The sun is serving the world with its heat and light, the moon is serving the world by exerting its pull on the oceans, the trees serve us by supplying our lungs with fresh oxygen, the rainclouds serve us by replenishing the earth and making it possible for us to live comfortably upon it—the list goes on. Service is the natural order of the universe. It is only natural that we, too, should serve. I challenge you to run an experiment. Perform a small service for a friend or relative and observe their reaction, then observe your own. By acting in alignment with our service-oriented nature, we are sure to feel a deep sense of happiness and satisfaction.

Simple Living, High Thinking

We must invest our energy somewhere. Most people think they'll be happiest when they direct it towards external objects. Try instead to direct your energy inwards; focus on trying to understand who you are and what life's ultimate purpose is. You will eventually find greater pleasure than any number of external stimuli can provide. Consider the following questions:

- Who am I when I am asleep?
- Where was I before I was born?
- What in me causes me to become angry?
- What's the point of getting angry?
- Why do I feel the emotions that overwhelm me?
- Where did all the people who have left the world go?

Considering the above questions can trigger deep introspection. By looking inward, you will come across many other dimensions of life that will stimulate your search. Our internal worlds are like vast oceans, infinitely deep and ever-serene. If we maintain proximity to this world of peace, we will be much less affected by the world around us. Consider spending more time in this safe zone and observe how your sense of equanimity increases even in the face of life's most difficult challenges.

3.2. LACK OF BELIEF IN ONESELF

We unconsciously try to imitate those who inspire us. There is no inherent problem in this tendency; in fact, it can help us evolve into who we want to be. In the midst of the evolution, however, we will fall short at times. Perhaps we won't immediately get the same results as our idol despite our best efforts to follow their lead. This experience may lead to the implantation of the weed of self-doubt in our heart. This self-doubt often manifests as an array of negative self-assessments that drag us down incessantly. We may hear our mind saying the following things:

- 'How come they can do it but I can't?'
- 'I can't break this bad habit no matter how hard I try.'
- 'I'll never become a good spouse.'
- 'I'm hopeless.'

In such moments, it is best to stop looking outward at what's going wrong on the surface and instead look inward and ask in what ways we can develop internally to achieve the results we desire. We often have enough people around us doubting us; why add another doubter to the mix?

Replace that negative internal monologue with positive, practical thinking.

- 'What can I do to move one inch closer to my goal?'
- 'This time, I made a mistake. I'll try again and make sure that pitfall is avoided the next time.'

- 'Failures needn't be detrimental; I'll make them the steppingstones to my ultimate success.'

Add some hard work and perseverance to these considerations and your ultimate success is assured. Never let the weed of self-doubt overcome your life's growth.

3.3. INDULGING THE URGE TO WASTE TIME

Most of us are all too familiar with the enemies of productivity: social media, streaming platforms, television, group chats, sensational news stories, gossip, etc. These weapons of mass distraction are perhaps the most violent killers of our potential. We may even be aware of this fact, but we still indulge ourselves. The fact is that these time-wasters can exert a vice-like grip on our consciousness. Just like gambling or smoking, it is easy for us to become addicted to those things that give us some semblance of pleasure or at least a sense of aloofness from life's pressures and responsibilities. Even if we think we are managing our usage well, at the end of the week, our device may tell us that we've spent hours immersing our consciousness in things that are ultimately a waste of time.

By nature, we are pleasure-seekers. If we can't find that pleasure within, we will be forced to search for it externally by doing the kinds of things mentioned above. That kind of pleasure ultimately leaves us feeling unfulfilled, so the solution is to find a more lasting, satisfying pleasure within ourselves. The way to do this is by building inner strength. By connecting with our spiritual side and finding happiness there, we can gain the strength required to say no to the false and time-killing pleasures of the screen.

Tips for Healthy Cell Phone Usage

1. Avoid checking your phone first thing in the morning. Instead, dedicate the early hours of your day to deep breathing, meditation, edifying literature, exercise and other things that will get you started on a positive note.
2. Avoid checking your phone for the last two hours of your day. This allows for more rejuvenating sleep and a better mood and heightened concentration the next day.
3. Silence unnecessary notifications like those related to social media and frivolous group chats.
4. Use apps that can increase your productivity and help you curb the time you spend on social media and other addictive applications.

5. Avoid using your phone during meals or while otherwise spending time with friends and family. Practise being completely present with those around you.
6. Establish a certain time of day when you check and respond to all emails and non-urgent messages.

3.4. POOR TIME ALLOCATION

To simply act without a proper schedule or plan is considered tamasic. The act of making a schedule is considered rajasic. To adhere to a schedule by living in a steady and regulated way on a daily basis is considered sattvic.

We have the tendency to overestimate our capabilities. For example, we may tell someone that we will meet them at 6 p.m., believing that we will finish work by 5 p.m., reach home by 5.15, get refreshed by 5.45 and drive to the venue in fifteen minutes, arriving right on time. We fail, however, to account for the various what-ifs that may befall us. We hit unexpected traffic and reach home by 5.30. Then our family member ropes us into what they assured us would be a quick conversation that ends up taking up another ten minutes. By the time we get refreshed and hop back into the car, it's already past the time when we were supposed to arrive, and, alas, we're over half an hour late. Of course, unforeseen things will occur from time to time that throw off our plans, but we should minimize their effect as far as possible. This means arranging our schedule in a way that accounts for such possibilities. It's always better to be ahead of schedule than behind.

This principle especially applies to our work as well. That extra time buffer we leave ourselves can help increase the quality of our work going forward. On how many occasions have we miscalculated a timeline and had to rush to finish a project? Such slip-ups decrease the quality of our output and increase our stress and anxiety. Instead, we should allocate time as generously as possible, so that we not only finish projects on time but also go over them with great care to ensure they are of the utmost quality. This kind of output is what will make us stand out and ultimately get ahead in our professional lives. So, there is no underestimating the power of proper time allocation.

3.5. POOR PRIORITIZATION

Effective prioritization is one of the major keys to time management. Poor prioritization is one of the gaping holes through which time escapes us. Almost everyone is very busy these days. We all have many tasks to perform on a day-to-day basis, but not every task is of equal importance. To be most effective, we must have a clear understanding of what should be done first and what can wait until later.

If we do not clearly identify what is to be done now and what is to be done later based on importance, the mind will often opt for the easiest tasks, leaving the more difficult (and sometimes more important) ones for later. By the time we get to the difficult tasks, we are already exhausted from our previous work, so we push them to the next day. This procrastination ultimately ends with our rushing through the important tasks in a state of anxiety; thus, quality is once again compromised. Consider the decision matrix we discussed earlier. If you keep the most important tasks at the forefront, you'll never have to worry about missing the mark.

3.6. OVER-EXTENDING (OR MISJUDGING ONE'S OWN AND OTHERS' ABILITIES)

Getting to know one's strengths and weaknesses is a lifelong process. For those especially introspective persons who are situated in the mode of goodness, that process is much faster. By coming to terms with who we are, we gain a better sense of those around us. For managers, this sense is of the utmost importance, for how can one properly engage their subordinates if they don't have a clear sense of what they can do? By having a good honest grasp of our team's capabilities, we can reach our full potential and consistently generate quality content. There is a story in the Ramayana that aptly captures the power of proper judgement.

After their queen was stolen away by an evil demon, a large group of monkeys gathered at the southern tip of India to discuss which of them would leap over the ocean to Sri Lanka to retrieve her. Each monkey, valiant by nature, suggested his own name and described his jumping expertise. Jambavan, their leader, had a perfect understanding of each one's ability. Upon some deliberation, he finally spoke: 'Hanuman is the biggest among us and he has the greatest jumping ability. He is the most suitable one for this task. Perhaps in my younger days I would've taken up the task, but Hanuman is the fittest among us. He should take the lead.'[14]

We may note that, although Jambavan could possibly have executed the task himself, he was humble and wise enough to know Hanuman was the best fit for the job. He therefore ignored the

14 Sundara Kanda, Ramayana

glory at stake and assigned the role to the right candidate. This is the mark of a true leader: the desire to make everyone around you better, *not* to exploit your team for your own aggrandizement. Expert managers thus clearly understand their own abilities and the abilities of those around them in an objective way and delegate work accordingly.

This kind of maturity and wisdom is absolutely required to not only optimize our time management but also maximize our potential in general. When we fail to properly assess our capabilities and those of others, we often wind up biting off more than we can chew and produce low-quality output. On top of that, our team's potential is stifled, and all parties collectively fall behind. As U.S. President Harry Truman said, 'It is amazing what you can accomplish when you don't care who gets the credit.'

3.7. RISING LATE

Benjamin Franklin once said, 'The early morning has gold in its mouth.'[15] In other words, if we

15 Joe Davis, 'The Morning has Gold in its Mouth', 24 July 2017, https://medium.com/@joethedave/the-morning-has-gold-in-its-mouth-66b59d128496#:~:text=Benjamin%20Franklin%20is%20quoted%20as,Acted%20upon%20them%3F

consistently rise early and maintain a regulated routine, we'll be amazed at what we can achieve. Make sure you knock out those big tasks first; that way, they don't bog you down later in the day. We also understand that the mode of goodness is most prominent during the early morning hours. This makes it most conducive for clearing our minds and setting a positive tone for the rest of our day. During this time, the mind is in its freshest and most attentive state. Take advantage of your augmented capabilities by tending to those important matters which would take a much greater toll if put off for later.

On the other side of the spectrum, the late evening hours are predominated by the mode of ignorance or the mode of darkness. This mode saps our energy and makes it harder for us to be productive. We also find that our discerning power is weakened. We may often find ourselves unable to make the right decisions, and making the wrong decisions can come back to bite us later. So, as far as possible, we should try to avoid carrying work over into these later hours.

I see many college students and youth cultivating the habit of rising very late in the morning. Their reason is that they prefer to work late at night, as they can focus during those hours. This may be fine during exams, but it is advisable not to make it a habit. Even if you are initially able to focus, you must recognize that you are being impelled by the mode of ignorance. People in the mode of ignorance are vulnerable to self-harming habits that lead to mental problems and are likely to make unwise decisions.

3.8. PROCRASTINATION (TAMAS)

We can always come up with an unlimited number of external reasons for putting something off, but internally speaking, there is usually just one root cause: the mode of ignorance (tamas). As previously mentioned, the mode of ignorance saps us of motivation, creativity and inspiration. It leaves us feeling like doing nothing, sometimes like we're *unable* to do anything. So, to optimize our time management, we should avoid habits that trigger

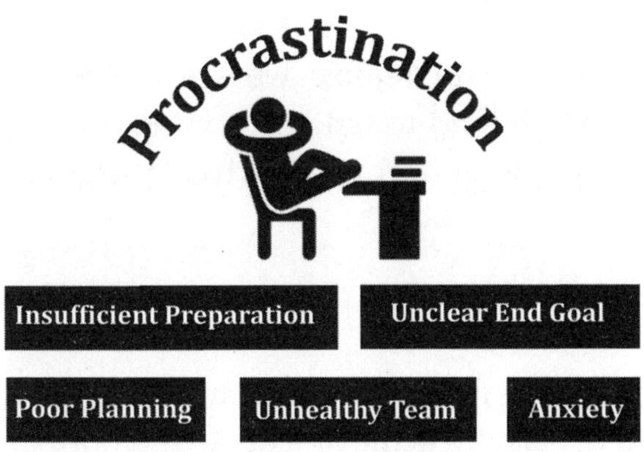

the mode of ignorance. These include oversleeping, watching mindless shows or sporting events and not properly maintaining our body with healthy food and exercise. By avoiding these triggers and instead maintaining more sattvic habits, such as regulating our sleep and ensuring that both our mind and body are being nourished with only the highest quality of inputs, we can take big strides in overcoming the pitfall of procrastination.

To completely eradicate the tendency altogether, however, we should also consider a few of the major external reasons why we may procrastinate. Let us take a deeper look at some of the roots of this undesirable weed.

Insufficient Preparation

Just as with planning, a failure to prepare is a preparation for failure. We have an innate sense of this. If we are scheduled to give a presentation or take a test but realize we are not sufficiently prepared, we tend to try postponing the occasion, preferring a potential breach of trust to a guaranteed failure.

Unclear End Goal

When we are not sure of the end goal, the steps we should take to achieve it are even more unclear.

Uncomfortable with the ambiguity and afraid of investing effort in the wrong areas, we tend to push the matter out of our minds entirely and hope it will sort itself out later on.

Unhealthy Team Relations

When it comes to group projects, if the team members are uncomfortable with each other, either because of unfamiliarity or because of negative experiences, communication will be stifled and, as a result, so too will the project itself.

Anxiety

If we are in an agitated mental state due to some unrest in our lives—perhaps family members' or our own health issues—we will not be able to work in an efficient and effective manner. The mind is the most important tool for any kind of work; if it is dulled, our work will suffer.

Poor Planning

If we do not divide our time up wisely, according to the importance and urgency of different sets of tasks, we will end up leaving ourselves plenty of time for petty tasks and no time for the most important ones. As those important tasks pile up and eventually overwhelm us, we're forced to postpone endlessly.

***

Do you recognize any of these causes for procrastination? I'm sure most of us have either personally experienced or otherwise witnessed their influence at play. Though each cause is distinct in its own way, there is one solution to all of them. By changing the way we carry ourselves and adopting a more sattvic lifestyle, all of the above factors can be nullified. By regulating our activities, becoming clearer about who we are and what our goals are, being more in tune with those around us and more even-minded and by understanding what is most important, we can bypass all of these pitfalls and maximize our productivity. Sattva is the panacea. We will discuss how to further cultivate this sattvic mentality in the sections to come.

3.9. THE MYTH OF MULTITASKING

We multitask all the time! Some examples of this would be eating while reading the news or talking to a friend while driving. Such things are second nature to us. But when the two activities we're attempting to combine demand more mental power than we're accustomed to exerting, problems are bound to set in. In complex situations where each detail is vital, is multitasking beneficial?

Let's consider a modern scenario. Say you're de-bugging a software program that needs to be in production and running in three hours. Meanwhile, you're on the phone with the test team about the ongoing testing procedures. At the same time, you're answering urgent emails from the end-users about the newly implemented system. Can you feel the pressure? How about the anxiety?

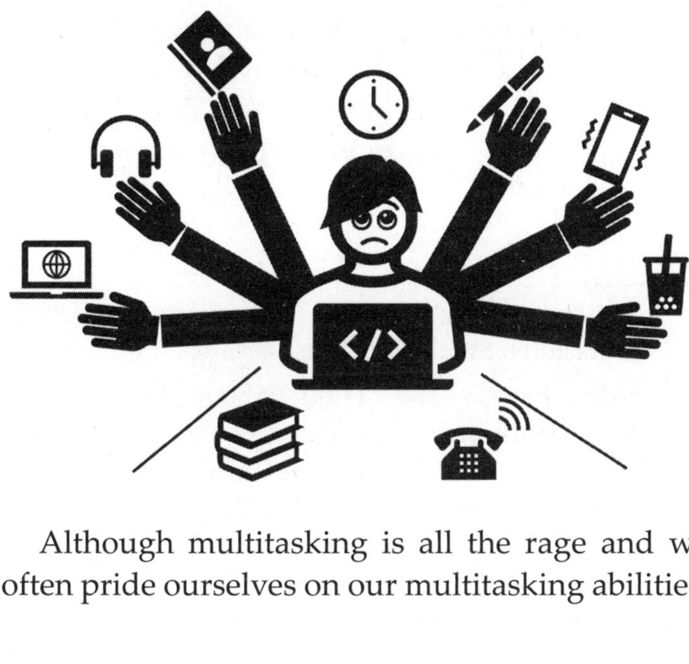

Although multitasking is all the rage and we often pride ourselves on our multitasking abilities, scientists have found that we can only *fully* focus on *one* thing at a time. Thus, although our style of work may give the appearance of heightened productivity, our ability to produce quality output diminishes with time.[16] To be exact, psychologist Susan Weinschenk says multitasking can dock our overall productivity by 40 per cent![17] By over-extending our cognitive ability, we lose cognitive power. MIT neuroscience professor Earl Miller says, 'Don't try to multitask. It ruins productivity, causes mistakes, and impedes creative thought. Many of you are probably thinking, "But I'm good at it!" Sadly, that's an illusion. As humans, we have a very limited capacity for simultaneous thought—we can only hold a little bit of information in the mind at any single moment. You don't actually multitask, you task-switch. This wastes time,

---

16 American Psychological Association. (2006). Multitasking: Switching Costs. *apa.org*.

17 Aprille Janes, 'The Truth About Multi-tasking And Creativity', *Aprille Janes Studio,* https://aprillejanes.com/truth-about-multitasking-and-creativity/#:~:text=Multi%2Dtasking%20makes%20me%20LESS%20productive&text=According%20to%20Dr.,as%20much%20as%2040%25

makes you error-prone and decreases your ability to be creative.'[18]

In today's world, focusing is already hard enough. Why set ourselves up for more difficulty than we're already bound to experience? Consider the magnifying glass. When focused on a single point, it can start a fire; however, if it is constantly moving from one thing to another, it won't affect any of those things. Our mental faculties are much the same. By focusing on one task at a time, our output and productive power reach their summit. Make sure you're putting your best cerebral foot forward by zooming your full awareness in on one important task at a time.

3.10. SCROLLING FOR RELAXATION

When we relax, we are meant to be recharging our minds and bodies. Endless browsing through social media and the web has the exact opposite effect. After some time, we start to feel even more lethargic, irritable, anxious and exhausted

18 Earl Miller, 'Multitasking: Why Your Brain Can't Do It and What You Should Do About It', Radius.MIT.edu, 11 April 2017, https://radius.mit.edu/programs/multitasking-why-your-brain-cant-do-it-and-what-you-should-do-about-it

than we were before. Not only is our energy depleted, countless hours are also wasted scrolling to oblivion. Subconsciously, our brain replays all that it witnessed in our endless scrolling, thus prolonging our depletion even further yet somehow keeping us stimulated enough to not be able to fall asleep.

In this way, our scrolling severely impairs us in the moment and afterwards, as we suffer from the effects of a lack of substantial rest. Instead of scrolling to relax, try activities that help rejuvenate the mind and body. These may include deep breathing, taking a nature walk, sneaking in a power nap, doing some meditation or yoga or reading an edifying book. When we engage in these restorative activities, our mind and body will thank us and so too will our boss, spouse, children and anyone else that we give our time and energy to.

3.11. CONCLUSION

In the last two chapters, we have gone over many of the obstacles that get in the way of optimal time management. To diligently avoid these impediments, we need to make both internal and external adjustments. Internally, we need to strive for sattva to develop discipline, enthusiasm, determination and spiritual well-being. Externally, we must diligently plan our tasks so that we can spend most of our time dealing with the second quadrant of important but not urgent activities. We must also split up our projects

into tasks and allocate sufficient time for each. We must then monitor our schedule on a weekly basis to make sure we are on the right track according to the goals we've established. We must also keep an eye on activities that waste our time. If we sometimes lose time as a result of such activities, instead of being overly hard on ourselves, we must instead learn our lesson and make sure we don't fall prey to them going forward.

SUMMARY

Major Obstacles When It Comes to Time Management

1. FOMO (Fear of Missing Out)
2. Lack of belief in oneself
3. Indulging the Urge to Waste Time

4. Poor time allocation
5. Poor prioritization
6. Over-extending
7. Rising late
8. Procrastination
9. Multitasking
10. Scrolling for relaxation

External Reasons for Procrastination

1. Insufficient preparation
2. Unclear end goal
3. Unhealthy team relations
4. Anxiety
5. Poor planning

QUESTIONS

1. Which activities hold you back from achieving maximum productivity? How will you overcome them?

____

____

____

____

2. Is FOMO affecting your time management and your life? How can you overcome FOMO?

____

____

____

____

CHAPTER 4

Time Management Techniques

4.1. TO-DO LIST

Many of the most successful people of the world are great planners. It is their heightened planning ability that allows them to accomplish more than most other people. By honing our personal planning power, we too can realize our full potential. If we take a look at our own lives, we'll notice that many of the things we do on a day-to-day basis can be automated so as to maximize our productivity. One of the easiest ways to ensure our days stay on track is to work based on a list. One of the biggest causes of time wastage is uncertainty regarding what to do next. By defining the tasks we seek to accomplish and thus having a set direction for our day, we enable ourselves to naturally flow towards achieving our goals.

Whenever an important task comes to our mind, we should immediately add it to our to-do list. This list can be on a piece of paper or in digital form, but it should be something we keep on us at all times so that each moment of the day can be assigned a place in our plan. In this day and age, to remember something means to write it down, no matter who we are. The CEO of a notable American non-profit told me of a huge residential building he had once acquired. After completing all the paperwork and weaving their way through endless red tape, he and his team finally closed the deal. Unfortunately, though it had crossed his mind at the moment of acquisition, he forgot to file the corresponding non-profit papers required to receive the tax benefits they were due. At the end of the year, he received a rude awakening in the form of a letter sent by the city requesting the extra funds owed.

Sometimes, a small pen works better than a big brain. Even the greatest minds among us are subject to forgetfulness. Instead of relying on our fallible memory, it might turn out to be much safer and more effective to just write things down. For all the ways a smartphone can hurt us, the to-do list is a big way in which it can help. By logging each important task we need to accomplish, we can rest easy knowing that we're not forgetting anything important. In this way, we save a lot of time and develop peace of mind. Our road to maximum efficiency does not end here, however. Just because we have a list of tasks at hand doesn't always mean we'll complete them in the most efficient manner. Let's take a look at how to not only get things done but how to do them well.

4.2. A FEW HOURS OF FULL FOCUS

> *Don't be fooled by the calendar. There are only as many days in the year as you make use of. One man gets only a week's value out of a year while another man gets a full year's value out of a week.*
>
> —Anthony Charles Richards

In today's world of mass distraction, many of us waste immense amounts of time without understanding the value of what we are squandering. We've all been there before: while hard at work, our concentration is suddenly snapped by a little *ting* sound. We break focus for a moment to check our phone and, before we know it, we've lost thirty minutes along with the whole flow we had going for us before the break.

We are subject to such disturbances all through the day, due to which we can end up going through many years without ever finding a strong flow of efficiency.

Instead of surrendering to the mediocre level of concentration that our phone may or may not afford us on any given day, it would be better for us to block out a few power hours in which we can fully maximize our output. Just like we work a certain event into our weekly schedule, we should similarly work these power blocks into our life. By ensuring we have at least one block of time a day in which we can *fully* focus on our work, we can set ourselves up for consistent leaps in progress and achieve a reliable flow of steady productivity.

Though we may not be able to completely dump our distractions, we can at least limit their influence upon us. By employing the power-hour technique, we can be sure we're making a daily investment in the path towards success, whatever our field. With such steady investments, we can actually watch ourselves making progress towards our goals. If time is money, it would only make sense that we regularly invest it for future returns. Let's see how else we can turn time spent into successful investments.

4.3. VALUE-TO-EFFORT RATIO

Investors in the corporate world typically expect returns in the range of 5–10x on their investments. In the same way, we should expect ample returns from the things we invest our time in. If the results we receive are meagre, we should consider altering our investment strategy. Just as investors use algorithms to decide which ventures are likely to be most profitable, we too can gauge our engagements' profitability with a simple equation:

If Value ÷ Effort > 1, we're good to go.

If Value ÷ Effort < 1, it's not worth your time.

If Value ÷ Effort = 1, change the strategy to improve the performance.

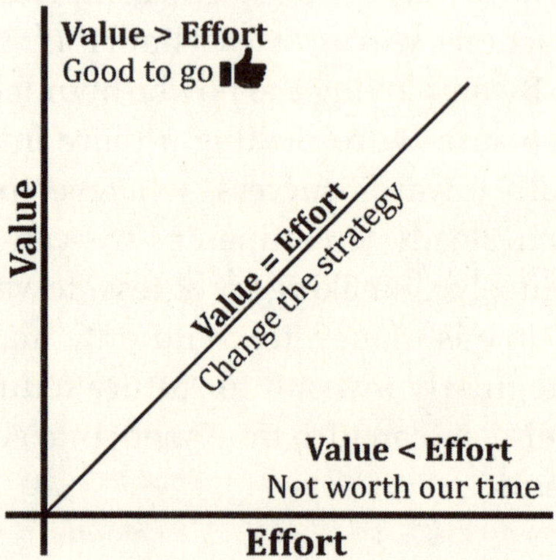

We can quantify value in many ways: annual revenue, cumulative financial assets, collection of data, customer satisfaction ratings, product output, etc. Our effort can be quantified in terms of the financial assets or time we invest.

We need to have systems in place to continuously monitor our value-to-effort ratio. So long as it is greater than 1, we are operating at an efficient level. If our value is equal to our effort, we must improve our efficiency by identifying and fixing the hole in our systems that's allowing value to leak out. If, on a regular basis, our value-to-effort ratio is less than 1 despite the adoption of various strategies and prudent changes, the endeavour is not worth our time.

Management consultant Dave Nicolette says we must maintain a detached, economic perspective on the time we are allocating to different projects. If we do not get sufficient value from the time we put in, then we should adjust our time allocation. If we don't, we will be doomed to continuously bleeding time and resources without any return significant enough to make up for our losses. Oftentimes, making adjustments to such a project is as simple as cutting out the aspects of it that may be expensive but ultimately ineffective.

Maximum efficiency demands a holistic approach. Whereas money managers invest solely for the sake of increasing monetary assets, we as humans must invest with a bigger picture in mind. Let's look at a few other investments we can make to ensure complete development, both inside and out.

4.4. INVEST FOR SUCCESS

> *The key is in not spending time, but in investing it.*
>
> —Stephen Covey

When people live without clear goals and aspirations or without a steady drive to achieve them, they tend to shell out much of their time to useless pursuits. Such people simply float around accepting whatever may come their way for better or worse. But if we have a strong desire to achieve something unique in this lifetime, we must invest time *now*. If we instead simply go with the flow and hope for our goals to fall into our lap, we're in for a rude awakening. Let's look at a few areas that we can invest our time in now for seamless success down the line.

Health

When we are sick, we lose a considerable amount of time trying to recover. Illnesses can totally wipe us out for days or even weeks on end. What does this tell us? That health is paramount. The best way to avoid illness is to boost our immunity. Some people consume a teaspoon of honey and lemon in the morning to this end. East Asians believe in the power of haritaki powder with honey while those in north India have a similar relationship with turmeric. Intermittent fasting also provides a number of health benefits that can pay dividends down the line. According to Johns Hopkins neuroscientist Mark Mattson, intermittent fasting has been proven to boost our memory and protect the body from diabetes, heart disease, inflammatory bowel syndrome and various forms of cancer. By investing in our health through the adoption of a disciplined lifestyle (good diet, sufficient sleep and regular exercise), we can achieve the best possible physical condition and are unlikely to lose time to illness.

Relationships

A large portion of our happiness comes from the affection we give and get. The affection we derive from our relationships makes up the real substance of our lives. Conversely, relationship problems can leave us bereft of both inner fulfillment and time. Amidst relationship struggles, we might end up barely sleeping and may even find our consciousness marred when we are kept awake by the stress and anxiety of the situation. Ensuring that we give proper attention and loving care to those in our circle will make us and those around us feel fulfilled and give us the freedom to work at a much higher capacity. Hence, we need to invest time in preserving, sustaining and enhancing our relationships. To qualitatively invest our time, we need to develop an attitude of service and gratitude. If we show appreciation and exhibit a supportive nature in our interactions, we can forge strong relationships. Empathic listening also helps in preserving relationships. We will discuss this topic in more detail in the anger management section.

Systematic Procedures

By devising specific procedures to complete given tasks in the most efficient manner, we save huge amounts of time that would otherwise have been wasted. Doing so in the workplace, especially amongst subordinates, also helps instil a sense of discipline that will yield even greater returns than the time saved alone.

For example, assembling a car consists of four major stages:

1. Build the chassis
2. Place the engine in the chassis
3. Attach the doors, wheels and hood
4. Paint the body

By developing a procedure that makes each stage more efficient, we can ensure that huge numbers of cars are produced in a reasonable amount of time. In the assembly line system, there are specially trained workers for each stage who are able to complete the tasks involved in that stage very quickly. They then pass on the product to the workers of the next stage, and so it goes. If each stage takes ten minutes and the workers in the first stage start on the second car as soon as they complete their work on the first, four cars can be produced in seventy minutes. In this way, efficiency can be maximized.

Systematic Procedure of Car Assembly

Build the chassis (10 min)	Fix the engine (20 min)	Attach the doors, wheels and hood (30 min)	Paint the car (40 min)

Systematic and Efficient Procedure of Car Assembly with Pipelining

Build the chassis (10 min)	Fix the engine (20 min)	Attach the doors, wheels and hood (30 min)	Paint the car (40 min)

Power Hours

As previously mentioned, if we block out certain hours for 'deep work', our efficiency skyrockets. No more will a phone notification turn into an hour lost. No more will a stray thought about checking something insignificant on the web break our workflow. By keeping the workflow steady, we make progress towards our goals. As mentioned earlier, some people prefer to work in the early morning because of the tranquillity in the atmosphere. For others, their optimal work time may be the late afternoon or evening. Ultimately, it is up to you. Find out your optimal work time and schedule power hours within it for big strides towards your goals.

Are you investing your time in something that really matters to you?

Do you have goals with timelines and schedules?

Are you treating your time as an asset to be invested for future returns?

Human life is precious, and it happens in a flash. How will you weave your life story as time goes on?

4.5. ONE MOMENT AT A TIME

Life is very interesting if you think about it. We go on, day after day, with no definite understanding of what the future will bring, never being able to undo what we've done in the past but, at the same time, capable of learning from our mistakes and evolving towards perfection. Each person crafts their life in their own way. Some shape their life like a waterfall, with endless thrilling jolts, jerks and crashes. Others prefer their life to be a serene stream that moves along, slow and steady. Still others prefer their lives to be like an ocean, with unlimited oceanic activity happening inside all the time. Regardless of the lifestyle one prefers, their life will ultimately be shaped by the choices they make on a moment-to-moment basis. What this often boils down to is the way we choose to react to the things life throws our way.

I once heard someone say that life is 10 per cent what happens to us and 90 per cent how we respond. Our life story is, in most cases, a long one. It is filled with all kinds of positive and negative experiences. However, if we are able to learn and grow from the negative experiences, then they too become transformed into positive ones. It is logical to choose growth over despair. After all, the past is already set in stone; once something has happened, the only power we retain is how we choose to let it affect us. We should utilize this supremely powerful present moment to create a wholly positive life story in which our apparent failures become the pillars that support our ultimate success.

P.A.S.T.A.: Transform Your Dreams into Reality

What is the difference between a dream that remains a dream and one that becomes a reality?

Often, it is not the size of the dream but the method one employs to achieve it that matters. There are always many possible paths to our goals, but wouldn't it be nice to know a few tried-and-true methods that you can plug into your life for definite progress? To this end, we've developed the P.A.S.T.A. strategy, based on proven techniques used by high achievers to turn dreams into realities.

P: Pen your dreams

A: Associate with high achievers

S: Strategize

T: Trash what doesn't work

A: Act enthusiastically from beginning to end

Pen Your Dreams

As soon as we write something down, our dream, which previously existed only on the subtle plane, becomes partially manifested in the physical world. If we then make a schedule of daily activities that aid in our progress towards our dream, we can watch as its degree of reality becomes more and more acute. We need only maintain a strict internal resolve to follow the schedule we've devised, always monitoring our progress as we advance towards our desired destination.

A notable proponent of this process was American founding father Benjamin Franklin,[19] whose many accomplishments shaped not only his life but those of all Americans to this day. Franklin adhered to an extremely strict schedule, in which his bedtime, wake-up time, work time and meal times were all fixed. At the end of the day, he'd always ask himself, 'What good have I done today?' Through perpetual progress and vigilant self-monitoring, Franklin would go on to become one of the most productive and prominent figures in American history.

Here are some questions you can ask yourself to catalyse the process of turning your dreams into reality:

1. Do I write down my goals along with a timeline for completing them?
2. What are my goals in the different areas of my life?
3. Why do I want to achieve them?

19 Benjamin Franklin, *The Autobiography of Benjamin Franklin* (Fingerprint! Publishing, 2015).

4. How will it make me feel when I achieve them?
5. What do I need to do *today* to achieve these goals? This week? This year?
6. Do I have a daily and a weekly schedule?
7. Am I sticking to my schedule?

Associate with High Achievers

There is a famous quote that goes, 'Show me your friends and I'll show you your future.' The people we associate with play a big role in what we do and, in turn, who we ultimately become. In many ways, we become who we associate with. Students at Ivy League colleges perform at a much higher level than most others, not just because of their natural intellect but also because of the competitive nature of Ivy league environments. There, it's *cool* to excel academically. At other schools, it is usually considered cooler to just have as good a time as possible and come to class still reeling from the night before. The results of both paradigms speak for themselves.

By associating with high achievers, we naturally become inspired to follow suit. It also gives us the opportunity to inquire and learn from them how they're able to get ahead. Conversely, if we associate with lazy people who prefer to coast through life without any drive, we will be subdued by their influence. We must be careful about who we associate with.

Ask yourself the following questions and consider how you can optimize the influences around you:

- What kind of people do I hang out with on a regular basis—performers or procrastinators?
- What do I learn from them?
- What can I do to inspire my peers?

Strategize

To act without a pre-meditated strategy is a recipe for failure. Our strategy shouldn't just be some ethereal idea but must take the form of a clear step-by-step path to success. To this end, we must allocate chunks of time to executing our plan on a weekly basis. By giving sufficient thought to these details, we can greatly limit the glitches that are bound to arise.

The approach of Jack Dorsey, founder of Twitter, is emblematic of the value of strategizing. Each of his work weeks was mapped out for years. Each day, he would spend eight hours working on a particular aspect of his company. Mondays were for management, Tuesdays for product development, Wednesdays for marketing and so on. Working for years in this way, Dorsey turned Twitter into one of the foremost online platforms in the world. What does your plan for success look like?[20]

Everyone knows that the early bird gets the worm, but the one that learns from that first bird's attempts and strategizes accordingly will get more worms in the end. A great example of this is Apple. In the early 2000s, many companies started releasing smartphones. Apple, however, did not. They instead watched their soon-to-be competition's moves, analysed their devices and developed a device and a marketing plan that would eventually make them the dominant player in the field. By studying the pitfalls and inadequacies of the smartphones of the time, they were able to craft a model that far exceeded the

20 Ellis Hamburger, 'You Won't Believe How Many Hours Jack Dorsey Puts in Every Day at His Two Companies', Yahoo News, 14 November 2011, https://www.yahoo.com/news/wont-believe-many-hours-jack-171506547.html

capabilities and personal feel of all others. The result? In the fourth quarter of 2021, Apple claims a 56 per cent market share of the US smartphone industry.[21]

One of the most powerful exhibitions of strategy known to man is that of nature. Its unique strategy can be observed as the seasons progress. In the hot summer, all the water from the land evaporates, slowly but surely forming massive rainclouds overhead. Upon the arrival of the rainy season, the clouds burst forth and drench the soil below, creating the perfect environment upon which crops may abundantly grow. Once fall comes around, the humidity

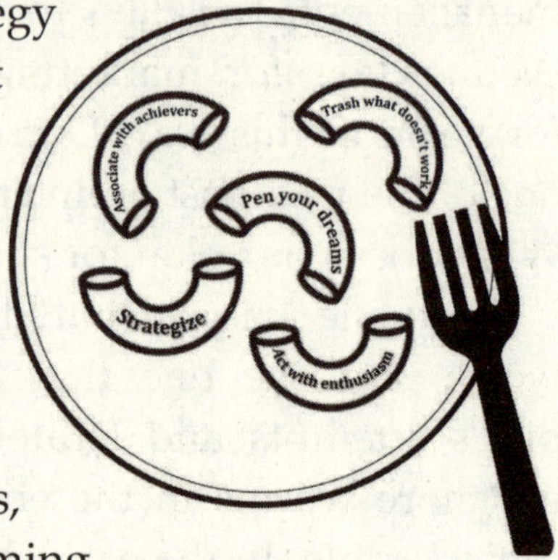

21 'A US Smartphone Market Share Report covering Q3 2020 – Q4 2021 shows a Clean Sweep by Apple', Patentlyapple.com, https://www.patentlyapple.com/2022/02/a-us-smartphone-market-share-report-covering-q3-2020-q4-2021-shows-a-clean-sweep-by-apple.html#:~:text=A%20new%20analytical%20report%20covering,competitor%20was%20Samsung%20at%2022%25

subsides, causing leaves to fall and mix with the earth, fertilizing the soil for the next year's harvest. This strategy provides enough crop for everyone to eat comfortably without any question of shortage. This is the power of a sound strategy! Just imagine the impact we can have on the world if we develop a powerful strategy of our own.

With this understanding in mind, ask yourself the following questions:

1. Do I have a strategy?
2. What kind of strategy can I employ to make systematic progress?
3. Am I courageous enough to implement it?

Trash What Doesn't Work

By vigilantly monitoring your progress, you get to know what is helping your development and what is not. After identifying those things that are detrimental to progress, we must cut them out of our lives to ensure our continuous development. In this way, we should constantly refine our process, making it progressively more efficient and effective. By accepting those things that favour our progress and rejecting those that don't, we can avoid stagnation and steadily advance towards our goals.

This refinement process may very nicely be applied to our personal lives as well. If we pick up a bad habit somewhere down the line that we know is not helping us become who we'd like to be, instead of idly allowing it to continue to hold us back, we should identify it as a detrimental tendency and cut it out. Through such vigilant refinement, we can watch ourselves progress along the path to personal perfection.

Act Enthusiastically from Beginning to End

Before starting a project, we should have an end goal in mind. Without this, it's very easy to become despondent when we face inevitable difficulties. By keeping this end goal in mind and recalling it whenever things go wrong, we can remain enthusiastic all along. With this enthusiasm, we will be able to cross all the hurdles and obstacles that appear in our path towards success.

Michael Jordan is a good example of someone who persevered with enthusiasm throughout his life. He was cut from his high school basketball team. He missed more than 9,000 shots in his career and lost almost 300 games. He was entrusted with the game-winning shot but missed it on twenty-six occasions. He failed repeatedly in his life but, with every failure, he kept going forward, learning from his failures with enthusiasm. He eventually succeeded and became a six-time NBA champion, a five-time NBA MVP (Most Valuable Player of the season) and a fourteen-time NBA All-Star.

Enthusiasm also gives way to two invaluable qualities: discipline and attention to detail. Enthusiasm is the fuel that allows one to stay the course and maintain one's standards when the going gets tough. Whereas others waver in their determination, the enthusiastic ones remain fixed and focused on the glorious end goal. Just as a kite requires a strong hold on it to remain in flight, we too require discipline to ensure our continued elevation. The enthusiastic hand is the one that is able to hold the string steady no matter how strongly the kite pulls. Are you meeting life's storms with enthusiasm?

Enthusiasm inspires one to pay attention to the details that apathetic souls would overlook. In the competitive world, it is those small details in the margins that end up making the biggest difference in terms of who gets ahead and who gets left behind. By maintaining an enthusiastic outlook, one can preserve their sensitivity to those things that matter in the march of progress. In this way, one can remain ever-vigilant, no matter how long the road may be.

> Ask yourself the following questions:
>
> 1. Do I have a clearly defined end goal in sight?
> 2. Do I clock my progress when I feel despondent?
> 3. Do I maintain my enthusiasm in the face of adversity?

***

By employing the P.A.S.T.A. principles, we transform ourselves from dreamers to achievers. We've now entered the space in which dreams become reality. Still, even as we march forward, we may sometimes feel that our work is taking up too much time. Perhaps we are now excelling in our professional life, but our personal life is withering due to a lack of time. Let us now take a look at how we can make every second count and get more done in less time.

4.6. SIX KEYS TO IMPROVING YOUR EFFICIENCY

To be efficient means to generate the maximum output using the minimum resources. The following are seven keys guaranteed to help maximize your efficiency.

Start Early

Benjamin Franklin once said, 'Early to bed and early to rise makes a man healthy, wealthy and wise.' Mark Twain later echoed this view when he said, 'Get your biggest and most important task done first in the morning.'

As we've discussed before, sattva or the mode of goodness is most prevalent in the early morning. This is the time when tranquillity and clarity are most easily accessible and our brain is in its most relaxed state. The morning hours provide the best opportunity for efficient and effective work.

To sharpen the mind even more, many people use these hours for meditation, prayer and yoga. Doing so puts the mind in a favourable state, allowing one to breeze through otherwise strenuous tasks.

1. Do you have any spiritual practices that strengthen your intelligence and calm your mind?

2. Are you committed to addressing your biggest and most important tasks first thing in the morning?

Prioritize

Our success will be based on our ability to effectively prioritize. The mind prefers to focus on the easy things. By so doing, however, we tend to either run out of time or not put our best effort in when the time comes for the more difficult and often more important tasks. Another aspect of prioritization is cutting out unnecessary mental engagements as far as possible to focus on things more conducive to your ultimate growth. This means cutting down on things like social media, gossip or other forms of chitchat via messaging apps and the like. Even if we do have trouble cutting out those things, by focusing on the most important tasks (MITs) first, we can ensure steady advancement in both our personal and professional lives.

Healthy Breaks

Scientific research has shown that we can't focus on a given task for more than two hours at a time. Of course, we can force ourselves to push on, but studies show that taking intermittent ten-minute breaks increases our efficiency and effectiveness drastically. It has been proven that taking breaks improves our decision-making ability. East Asian companies advocate post-lunch power naps to rejuvenate the body and mind. Others advocate going for a nature walk to clear the mind before getting back to work. This powerful technique can be likened to sharpening an axe before chopping a tree. Don't work with a blunt axe.[22]

Time Allocation

Any good manager knows that, in order to get things done, he or she needs to allocate the proper amount time to the tasks at hand and then monitor the progress of a given project and allocate more or less time to it depending on how it's developing. Why not apply the same technique in our own life? If you want to get things done in your personal or professional life, allocate time to those things and monitor how your efforts are progressing.

22 Anangsha Alammyan, 'The Science of Taking Breaks at Work to Help Boost Your Productivity', Medium.com, 27 October 2020, https://medium.com/mind-cafe/the-science-of-taking-breaks-at-work-to-help-boost-your-productivity-ec3e1f47c818

Don't Take on Too Much

By applying the previous principle of allocating time to important things, much progress can be made, the only caveat being that, if we take on too many important things, our effectiveness in all areas will be greatly reduced. When we over-extend ourselves, we become prone to stress and irritability and our output suffers as a result. For this reason, we should become familiar with our limits and learn when to say no to new tasks or projects.

Strong Work Relationships

If we forge good bonds with our colleagues, work becomes more enjoyable. That connection also produces a strong synergy that propels the team's overall efficiency and productivity. Raymond Meredith Belbin, a British researcher and management consultant, contended that, often, the teams that wield the most intellectual prowess end up also being the most stagnant in meeting their goals. Without the right team spirit, an abundance of intellect can be stifling. The team that works with respect for one another and a common goal in mind is the better bet.[23]

---

23 'The 9 Belbin Team Roles and What They Accomplish', Qualitygurus.com, https://www.qualitygurus.com/the-9-belbin-team-roles-and-what-they-accomplish/

Cultivating mutual respect and a shared vision is a subtle thing. Let us take a quick look at how we can develop the synergy required to maximize our team's productivity. Rupa Goswami[24] , a fifteenth century bureaucrat-turned-saint, suggested six ways we can establish productive relationships: sharing gifts, sharing a meal, revealing one's mind in confidence and making confidential inquiries.

Sharing Gifts

Simple enough: this principle refers to the act of giving and receiving gifts. It is not so much about the gift itself but the expression of goodwill that the act carries with it. The act of giving a gift indicates that you value the person enough to give them something that costs you in some way. The more the selflessness with which the gift is given, the stronger the relationship will grow. That act of giving is powerful in that it creates a familial mood at the workplace; by learning how to channel it, you can be a conduit for positive relationships all year round.

Sharing Meals

A strong and lasting relationship often begins with an invitation to lunch or dinner. It is through such

24 Gosvami, *The Nectar of Instruction*

experiences that we get to know a person better and develop a more intimate connection with them. In America, corporate culture has recognized this by implementing weekly team lunches. However, the most powerful way to forge this bond is to actually invite someone into your home and share a home-cooked meal with them. This is a uniquely intimate experience that reinforces the goodwill and care felt within a given relationship.

Revealing the Mind in Confidence

Once an initial sense of security has been cultivated, it is natural for more intimate details to be exchanged between two people. This is done in confidence, with the sense that the other person values you enough to respect your privacy and not share what you've told them with whoever they feel like. The very act of sharing such details helps deepen the relationship, but it also simultaneously provides the relationship a unique opportunity to grow abundantly stronger: by making the conscious choice to not share with anyone else what the person has told us, we not only do the right thing but also make a long-term investment in the overall success of the connection. By failing to do so, we cap the potential of the relationship at a very shallow level and run the risk of damaging it beyond repair.

Making Confidential Inquiries

Making inquiries is another aspect of relationship-building. When we ask someone about or for information that is of particular value to us, we let them know that we value their opinion and that we trust them. This is another way to move a relationship to a more intimate level.

***

Relationship-building is akin to travelling on a frozen lake. We never run with wild abandon but always tread very carefully, making sure the ice below our feet is solid before taking the next step. Through such steady vigilance, we eventually come to trust the surface beneath us and then move more freely, with confidence. In the same way, as we get to know a person and gradually gauge their trustworthiness, we become more and more comfortable with letting down our guard. Genuine affection and service act as favourable breezes that push us along on this journey of interpersonal discovery. Consider how you can apply these four principles in a relationship you wish to deepen.

4.7. ORGANIZE TOMORROW TODAY

We know that by failing to plan, we plan for failure. The converse is also true—by succeeding at planning, we plan for success! Instead of wasting our precious morning hours on trying to figure out what we have to do and when we should do it, we can prepare the day's schedule before going to bed the previous night. That way, we have everything sorted for us when we wake up and can hit the ground running each and every morning, thereby maximizing our efficiency.

While planning your tomorrows, make sure you delegate the tasks you can and set reasonable timeframes for your activities. If you strictly adhere to your schedule and refrain from being distracted by your phone or letting meetings turn into prolonged chitchat, you'll be amazed by the number of things you can accomplish in a day. Let's take a deeper look at how we can refine our schedules for maximum effect.

The schedule refinement process consists of three stages:

1. Make the schedule
2. Monitor the schedule
3. Manage the schedule

Make the Schedule

Prepare a daily schedule shaped by the considerations mentioned above. There are many apps that can help us prepare our schedule.

Monitor the Schedule

After adhering to our daily schedules for one week, we should take a moment to reflect on how things have gone. Which activities took up most of our time? How can we delegate our time to new projects while ensuring the ongoing ones aren't being left behind? How much time did we lose on wasteful activities like social media scrolling? Still low on time? How much more time will you have to accomplish your goals if you cut down on wasteful activities? Ask yourself these questions as a way of refining your schedule continuously.

Manage the Schedule

Now it is time to take action and augment your schedule based on what you've observed. This is where we recognize the things in our day that hold us back from reaching our full potential—and eliminate them. These could either be obvious things like the time-wasters previously mentioned or more subtle things like overworking our mind to the point of dulling its edge.

Relaxation time can be just as important as work time if employed properly. If we don't give the mind and body time to rest and rejuvenate, we will run the risk of capping our maximum work potential due to exhaustion and fatigue. Let's take a look at a few ways we can make sure our tools stay sharp.

4.8. SELF-CARE ACTIVITIES

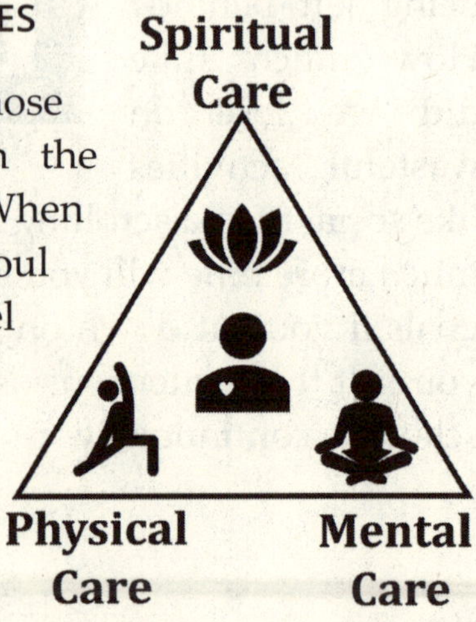

Self-care activities are those activities that nourish the body, mind and soul. When our body, mind and soul are in harmony, we feel healthy and happy. When the body is healthy but the mind is distressed, we feel holistically impaired, and the same is true of times when the mind is well but the body is sick. Let us take a look at some activities that can combine to ensure our complete well-being.

Physical Care

1. Healthy diet
2. Sufficient sleep
3. Physical exercise
4. Yoga
5. Pranayama (meditative breathing)
6. Bathing daily
7. Time in/with nature
8. Power naps
9. Staying hydrated
10. Sunlight

Mental Care

1. Meditation
2. Mindfulness
3. Listening to music
4. Practising sense control
5. Cultivating humility and respect for all
6. Positive interactions with others

Spiritual Care

1. Prayer
2. Mantra meditation
3. Service to others
4. Listening to wisdom
5. Introspection
6. Reading spiritual books

4.9. S.M.A.R.T. GOALS

To effectively manage our time, our goals need to be S.M.A.R.T.

S: Specific

Our goals should be very specific, with clearly defined outcomes. This means asking the following questions:

1. What exactly is the goal?
2. Who is involved in achieving it?
3. Where is the physical space in which we will be working towards it?
4. Why are we doing it?
5. When are we doing it?

M: Measurable

Our goals should be measurable. That way we can check whether we have achieved our targets. For this reason we need to definitively quantify our goal so that we can track our progress and assess our performance. For example, let us print 5,000 time management books a month for the next three years.

A: Attainable

Our goal should push the envelope in some way—it shouldn't be too easily attainable, but it should be something we can logically see ourselves accomplishing in our allotted timeframe.

Example: *We will increase the 'positive attitude' book sale by 20 per cent every year for the next three years.*

R: Relevant

Our goal should be in line with our values and our ultimate desired direction in life.

Example: *We should have 400 students enrolled in our yoga and mindfulness training by June 1.*

T: Timely

We should set a reasonable target date by which to accomplish our goals.

Example: *Organize a five-day yoga retreat in Miami, Florida, in December next year.*

4.10. MONK'S 'LOTUS LEAF' TIME MANAGEMENT TECHNIQUE

Our employers expect us to be efficient cogs in the machine, generating consistent results all year. Family members, on the other hand, expect us to give them our time, love and affection. Unfortunately, a lapse in one area tends to affect the other. Problems at work tend to strain our family relationships and problems at home can take a toll on our professional abilities. The questions that then arise are: how can we maintain a high level of

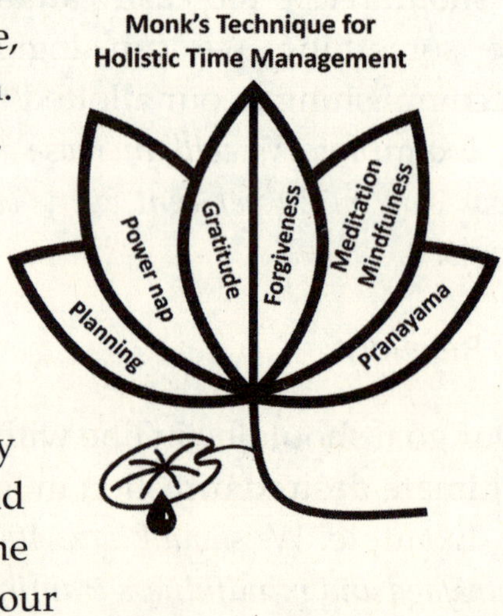

interpersonal availability when things go wrong at work and how can we maintain our professional output when dealing with issues at home? For consistency across the board, we can employ a technique that monks use when the going gets tough.

The lotus leaf technique is meant to help us attain a state of equilibrium. It was developed based on years of experience in training students, professionals and corporate leaders. The practices themselves are born of a marriage between the ancient eastern wisdom texts and modern western social experiments.

To use the lotus technique, one must follow these seven steps each day:

1. Before beginning your work, practise the *pranayama* breathing technique: deep inhalations and exhalations for five minutes. This is a scientifically studied procedure that has neurocognitive, psychophysiological, biochemical and metabolic advantages and promotes general health and well-being.
2. Employ a simple meditation and mindfulness technique: focus on your breath as it comes and goes. Become aware of your breathing. All the while, become comfortable with

being in the present. Don't follow any thoughts into the past or future.

3. Practise forgiveness. Let go of any ill will you harbour against anyone from the day before. Remember, no one is perfect, we all make mistakes and everyone is fighting their own difficult battles.
4. Practise gratitude. Be grateful for the work you've been given in this life and for the opportunity you have to make the most of the day ahead.
5. When you take a break for lunch, repeat the first four steps.
6. Towards the end of the workday, before you leave your workplace, prepare your work schedule for the next day.
7. Before bed, repeat the first four steps again while sitting in a secluded place.

Lotus leaves are known for their ultrahydrophobicity. In other words, they're known for being unaffected by water. Any drops that fall on them bead up and roll off onto the ground below. In the same way, we can become like the lotus plant by consciously fortifying our mind and consciousness with these special techniques. This allows us to be less influenced by life's inevitable storms and retain our own personal state of equilibrium no matter how strong the rain is.

4.11. PRIORITIZE YOUR MITS

What is currently your most important task (MIT)?

Generally, our most important areas of time allocation will fall amidst the trinity of career, relationships and legacy. Once we begin navigating our life between the lines of that triangle, our priorities become clear.

If you are changing your career, learning new and relevant skills may be your MIT.

For a junior in high school, mastering the math section of their upcoming SAT exam may be their MIT.

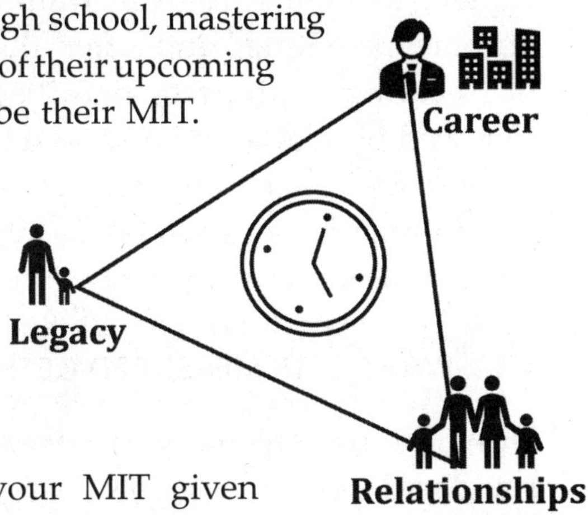

For a CEO, preparing for tax season and meeting with their accountant may be their MIT. What is your MIT given your current status and where you want to go?

Regardless of who we are and what our goals may be, we should allocate at least one hour each day towards taking care of our MITs. Some professionals dedicate 50 per cent of their working hours to their MITs. The actual hours and percentages will always vary based on an individual's given situation, but one should never let a workday go by without tending to one's most important tasks.

It's also worth noting that, while our general goals will stay the same for some time, our MITs are always subject to change. For example, an entrepreneur looking to open their own yoga and wellness centre may first view developing their courses as their MIT. Afterwards, their MIT will become patenting, and after that is taken care of, securing a property may become their MIT, followed by marketing and so on. In this way, we must remain on our toes, always ready to recognize and embrace the next MIT so as to steadily progress towards achieving our goals.

4.12. WHAT GETS MEASURED GETS DONE

How do we ensure we're working at a high standard?

As important as getting tasks done is monitoring our levels of efficiency on a weekly basis. A car may feel like it is running fine, but it must be inspected regularly to ensure there's nothing going on that could lead to a major issue down the road. In the same way, we should have a means by which we can measure our ultimate progress towards our goals and ensure all components of our work are well-oiled and ready for the long haul. To be able to gauge this, we can use key performance indicators (KPIs).

KPIs are bits of data we can monitor to objectively discern our levels of efficiency and progress. There are many useful KPIs whose applicability depends on the field of work in question. Someone who is writing a book can use the number of pages being written per week as a strong KPI. For a software consultant working in production support, a KPI could be the number of tickets they're able to solve per day. A KPI needn't be purely numerical; for a coffee shop owner, the week's cumulative customer satisfaction rating could be an effective indicator. Failing to take note of these bits of information is like failing to see the holes in our boat until we're already sinking. By recognizing our fallacies and responding with care, we can sail all the way to our desired shore.

4.13. BIOLOGICAL PRIME TIME

Our motivation, energy levels and focus don't remain constant through any workday; they fluctuate based on our environment and our own personal internal clock. By carefully observing ourselves and taking note of our own fluctuations throughout the day, we will be able to nail down our own personal biological primetime: the time at which we personally operate at peak performance. Conversely, we can also identify those times of the day when we are least effective. By scheduling our most important tasks into our primetime slots and scheduling breaks and rests during our least productive slots, we can maximize our overall output and always ensure we're playing to our strengths.

4.14. THE PARETO PRINCIPLE: THE 80/20 RULE

Vilfredo Pareto[25] was an Italian economist who observed that 20 per cent of the pea pods in his garden produced 80 per cent of the peas. After conducting research, Pareto applied this principle to macroeconomics, showing that 80 per cent of the wealth in Italy was owned by 20 per cent of the population. According to this principle, 80 per cent of all outputs or outcomes come from 20 per cent of all inputs or causes. Non-profit organizations

25 Vilfredo Pareto, Wikipedia, https://en.wikipedia.org/wiki/Vilfredo_Pareto

observe this principle in fundraising: 80 per cent of the funds come from 20 per cent of the donors, with the remaining 20 per cent of funds coming from 80 per cent of the donors.

Dr Joseph Juran, a management guru, further developed the 80-20 rule in terms of quality control. His research showed that 80 per cent of product defects were caused by 20 per cent of the problems in production methods. He asserted that if the relevant 20 per cent of production problems were eliminated, product quality would increase drastically. He called this with a phrase 'the vital few and the trivial many'.[26]

How do we apply the 80-20 rule to our life?

We need to focus on the 20 per cent of activities and/or people that produce the most results in our life, both intrinsically and at an observable level. By identifying this information and investing our energy appropriately, we can maximize our output, efficiency and satisfaction.

---

26 Louis Lobo, 'Pareto Principle: 80/20 Rule for Productivity—To Maximize Results', Medium.com, 29 September 2021, https://medium.com/@Thelouis/pareto-principle-80-20-rule-for-productivity-7d933f4fc11d#:~:text=He%20demonstrated%20that%2080%25%20of,few%20and%20the%20trivial%20many.%22

4.15. THE POMODORO TECHNIQUE

Managing our efficiency can also be enhanced by utilizing a time management technique developed by Francesco Cirillo in the late 1980s. Here is how his simple method works.

We split up our work into smaller bits and work continuously for twenty-five minutes (one 'pomodoro'), after which we make a check mark on our tracking sheet and take a short break of two to three minutes. We then continue working in the same manner until we have completed four pomodoros, approximately two hours. Here we can take a longer break of fifteen to thirty minutes in order to review our task. The main point is to devote undivided attention during a pomodoro and not be distracted by anything.

Here is a simplified version you can try:

Set a timer for 25 minutes and work on a task uninterruptedly. When the timer rings, stop the work. Put a tick mark on a sheet of paper and take a break for two to three minutes before beginning again. After four pomodoros, take a break of fifteen to thirty minutes in which you review your work. Continue the loop until the task is complete.

Customization of the Pomodoro Technique

Using a timer helps us focus and work with undivided attention. This can build determination and discipline, allowing us to accomplish more. The quality of our work can increase further if we recap and review our work after each pomodoro.

Personally, after four pomodoros, I engage in mantra meditation, disconnecting from my work and my surroundings and connecting with my soul's sacred space. This rejuvenates me and provides me with the energy required to keep working. Find a pomodoro technique that works for you and watch your energy and productivity soar.

4.16. CONSIDER EACH MINUTE

Let me echo some of the points mentioned earlier in this section to reiterate the importance of saving time.

Time is very precious. Yesterday is gone forever, so we must make the most of today. In the present-day world, we're faced with numerous weapons of distraction. One notification bell is all it takes to send us into another world for hours on end. First, we see the message, then we notice an interesting news headline below it and we click on it and are reminded of something else we wanted to look into, and before we know it an hour has been wasted, never to return. These instances add up in a day, a week, a month, a year. How much time do you think you've wasted on your phone in this lifetime? How much more will you waste? This scary reality highlights the need to recognize the value of each minute and the correspondingly detrimental nature of time-wasting activities. How can we avoid time-wasting habits? Let's take a look at a few things to keep in mind:

- **Important items**

  By keeping important items in a fixed place, we avoid the hassle of having to continually searching for them.

- **Important documents**

  If they are electronic, we can create folders or save them on the cloud. Physical documents can be filed alphabetically in a file box.

- **Interruptions**

  By working in chunks of dedicated time, we can be productive. People who go to the office very early often accomplish more.

- **Too much workload**

Organizing our work into modules can help in avoiding this problem. Also, not taking on more than we can handle or learning to delegate work can also prove effective. Learn to say no to others and focus on the most important things in your life.

- **Procrastination**

  Using a planner or a calendar to schedule tasks can help us follow through with our plans.

- **No priorities**

  Not having a fixed schedule or agenda is a sure-fire way to be susceptible to others' suggestions. We can easily become a 'yes man' to others' needs. By being clear about our priorities beforehand, we can make it easier for ourselves to say no.

- **Laziness**

  It is important to associate with people who are enthusiastic to perform.

Rupa Gosvami cautioned us not to waste even a minute, as death may come at any time and take everything away.[27]

27 Gosvami, *The Nectar of Instruction*

Practical Tips

1. Plan weekly, prioritize daily.
2. Allocate a minimum of an hour a day to your MITs.
3. Cut out unnecessary conversations and long phone calls or Zoom calls. With your goals in mind, utilize each minute efficiently.
4. Develop responsible smartphone habits. Failing to do so could be ultimately detrimental.
5. Don't waste time on social media or video games.
6. Avoid complaining about others. Complaining is a sign of immaturity.
7. Avoid long meetings. Stick to a solid agenda.
8. Never waste your time on the not important and not urgent things in the fourth quadrant.
9. Recognize the supremely valuable nature of time. Consider the following poem (whose author is unknown) in this connection:

   To gauge the value of one year, ask a student who failed their annual exams.

   To gauge the value of one month, ask a mother who gave birth to a premature baby.

> *To gauge the value of one week, ask the editor of weekly magazine.*
>
> *To gauge the value of one day, ask a daily wage labourer who has five kids to feed.*
>
> *To gauge the value of one hour, ask the lover who awaits their beloved.*
>
> *To gauge the value of one minute, ask a person who missed their train.*
>
> *To gauge the value of one second, ask a person who survived an accident.*
>
> *To gauge the value of one millisecond, ask an Olympic silver medallist.*

Let us make the most of each and every moment, lest we are filled with regret in the end.

4.17. A GOOD NIGHT'S REST

The Bhagavad Gita says we are not the body but a spirit soul.

We can compare our body to a machine which is more complex and intelligent than a modern electric car. If we understand this, then we must also understand the importance of getting a good night's sleep to rejuvenate and replenish the body. Our body is designed to heal and reconstruct while we sleep. Sleeping for a minimum of six to eight hours at night can facilitate the restoration and revitalization of all parts of our body.

Our body, just like the natural world outside of us, is made up of five natural elements: earth, water, fire, air and ether. According to ayurvedic wisdom, by following nature's cycle, we can stay healthy. For instance, our digestion is directly connected to the movements of the sun. When the sun is high (around noon), our digestive fire is most powerful. Therefore, by eating our heavier meals in the middle of the day and our lighter meals at night, we give our body the chance to more properly digest and absorb the nutrients in whatever we have eaten. Eating our dinner two to three hours before we sleep gives our body ample time to digest it; otherwise, our body will have to digest food while we are sleeping, causing us to experience a disturbed sleep. When we get up, we will feel tired.

Ayurveda also indicates that each hour of sleep before midnight is equal to two hours of sleep. After 4 a.m., every one hour of sleep is equal to only half an hour of sleep. Our body starts to regenerate and heal after 9 p.m. Therefore, sleeping late at night can reduce our body's ability to naturally rejuvenate and greatly impede our recovery from illness.

Another established fact is that blue light, emitted by electronic screens, is very detrimental to sleep. Our brain's release of melatonin (which promotes sleep) is inhibited by blue light. Refraining from using electronic gadgets one or two hours before sleep gives us the chance to enjoy better rest. Also, physical exercise, like yoga or walking during the day, helps improve the quality of our sleep at night.

Without a good night's sleep, our body does not recover from the fatigue of the previous day, thereby affecting our next day's performance. For better time management, a good night's sleep is imperative.

SUMMARY

Six Ways to Improve Our Efficiency

- Start work early
- Prioritize
- Allocate proper time slots for each task
- Take scheduled work breaks
- Maintain good relationships with colleagues
- Don't over-extend yourself

Strong Work Relationships

- Sharing gifts
- Sharing meals

- Revealing your mind in confidence
- Making confidential inquiries

S.M.A.R.T. Goals

- **S**pecific
- **M**easurable
- **A**ttainable
- **R**elevant
- **T**imely

Lotus Leaf Time Management Technique

Use this technique to improve your productivity.

QUESTIONS

1. Are you preparing S.M.A.R.T. goals for yourself?

____

____

____

____

2. Have you written down a few MITs and prepared timelines for their completion?

____

____

____

____

3. How can you apply the Pareto principle to your life?

____

____

____

____

4. How can you practically apply the lotus leaf technique to your life?

____

____

____

____

A Note on Sources

All references to religious writings, stories and myths have been taken from the Ramayana, Mahabharata, Bhagavada Gita and Bhagavata Purana, which have been accessed by me in the original Sanskrit. The translation from Sanskrit is my own.

The several quotations in the book have been taken from https://www.goodreads.com/ and https://www.brainyquote.com/.

Yugal Kishore Das

Acknowledgements

I am immensely grateful to my beloved Guru Radhanath Swami, who is the guiding light in my life.

I am grateful to Shyamananda Das from Chowpatty Temple for his support and guidance. I sincerely thank Gauranga Das for his wisdom and inputs on *Anger Management*; Radheshyam Das for his inputs on *Stress Management*; Chaitanya Caran for his suggestions and comments, especially with the book titles.

I sincerely thank Harsha Vardhan Chitta for his encouragement, without which this series would not have come into existence. He has been pushing me to write for the past ten years. He constantly supported this project by providing many much-needed resources. I am grateful to him and his wife Manasa for their warmth and affection.

I am immensely thankful to Prof. Ramana Vinjamuri for his inputs and guidance. He invested his precious time, energy and talent in all the phases of the project. He was involved at every step and in all the important decisions. He drew all the illustrations used in the books and also conceived and designed all the covers. I am deeply grateful to him and his wife Deepti for their continued support in my life. I sincerely thank Dr Shrawan Chittor Surender for his inputs and guidance on this project. I am very grateful to him and his wife Shilpa Surender for their constant support.

I am also grateful to Anupama Das for editing this book. He also many valuable suggestions to make the content appealing.

My sincere thanks goes out to the following: Dr Atul Kapoor, MD (Physician), and Dr Anisha Kapoor, MD (Physician), for their medical advice on *Stress Management*; Dr Kavitha Vasu, MD (Psychiatry), for her time and valuable suggestions on all three books; Dr Alka Desai, MD (Psychiatry), for her inputs on *Anger Management* and *Stress Management*; Dr Padmaja Vuppala, MD (Psychiatry), and her daughter Anusha; Dr Padma Morisetty, MD (Physician), and Dr Uma Pittala, MD (Physician); Dr Dan Fink MD (Physician); Dr Adria Savino, MD (Psychiatry).

I sincerely thank Dr Raman Chopra and his wife Dr Vanita Chopra for their support and encouragement.

I am grateful to my father (late) Satyanarayana Murthy Poolla for his love and affection mother Saraswathi, brother Veerraju, sister Rajyalakshmi for their affection and support throughout my life.

Thanks are also due to Nanda Niketan, Shyam Kishore, Bhagavat Acharya, Sundarhari, Shyamananda Krishna, Ravi Morisetty and Ram Tulasi for their support.

I extend my thanks to HarperCollins for publishing this book. I am grateful to Rakesh Chander and Hina Khajuria and their team, as well as our literary agent Dipti Patel to have made this project a pleasant reality.

And, finally, thanks to all of you readers who accepted the contents of these books with a graceful heart.

About the Author

Yugal Kishore Das is a globally renowned speaker, monk, lifestyle mentor, and coach. He holds a masters degree in mathematics, and bachelors degrees in science and law from various Indian universities. He has also studied software programming.

He is based in Michigan, but has travelled all over the US, imparting spiritual insights on work–life balance, relationships and mindfulness. He has also travelled widely to East Asia, the

Middle East and Europe, conducting seminars on personality development and providing guidance to students, professionals and corporate leaders. He has conducted seminars at universities such as Carnegie Mellon, University of Pittsburgh, University of Cincinnati, Wayne State University and Lawrence Tech University. He has also held seminars for multinational corporations like Procter & Gamble and Ford Motor Company, among others.

His goal is to build like-minded communities and equip them with the tools to address the problems of the modern world and toxic work culture. He believes that people can live in peace and harmony with nature if they have the right tools and support.

Please visit www.yugalkishore.com for more information, and to reach out to the author, please mail at contact@yugalkishore.com.